LAWRIE SANCHEZ

The Northern Ireland Years

HEATHER JAN BRUNT

First published in 2007
by Appletree Press
The Old Potato Station
14 Howard Street South
Belfast BT7 1AP

Tel: +44 (0) 28 90 24 30 74
Fax: +44 (0) 28 90 24 67 56
E-mail: reception@appletree.ie
Web: www.appletree.ie

A catalogue record for this book is available from
the British Library.

Lawrie Sanchez – The Northern Ireland Years

The moral right of the author has been asserted.

ISBN: 978 1 84758 061 0

Desk and Marketing Editor: Jean Brown
Editorial work and Design: Echelon Publishing Services
Cover Design: Stuart Wilkinson
Production Manager: Paul McAvoy

9 8 7 6 5 4 3 2 1

AP3499

CONTENTS

ACKNOWLEDGEMENTS

Thanks are due to a number of people:

First and foremost to Lawrie Sanchez without whom, clearly, this book would not have been written. This is not a biography of Lawrie – that story, with so much still to come, is for another day. This is a celebration, written from my own perspective, of his glorious years as manager of Northern Ireland. Inevitably some of the narrative focuses on the communications and media aspects of international football, as that was my area of responsibility within Team Northern Ireland.

When I first considered writing this book I sought Lawrie's permission and if it had not been forthcoming I would have discarded the idea. It was, and for that I am most grateful. In addition Lawrie gave me his full cooperation, speaking at length over several weeks to recall his own personal memories of these times.

Thanks are also due to the photographers whose work appears in these pages: especially William Cherry of Presseye who supplied the majority of the images, including the front cover; and Gary Hancock a freelance photographer and co-founder of the Amalgamation of Northern Ireland Supporters Clubs. William and Gary were both extremely generous in spending so much time searching through their collections to provide such an incredible selection of pictures.

I would also like to record my thanks to my former Irish Football Association colleagues David Currie and William Campbell for patient and continuous help with fact checking; to Mel Goldberg of Statham Gill Davies for legal expertise; and to Jean Brown of Appletree Press for calm and generous support during the copy-editing and proofreading stages.

Finally, my thanks are extended to every single person who agreed to be interviewed for this book, for sharing their own unique and warm memories of a very special time, enabling me to produce an in-depth record of Team Northern Ireland.

PREFACE

The Irish Football Association (IFA) is the fourth oldest association in world football and as a member of the International Football Association Board is one of the guardians of the laws of the game sitting as an equal with the other British associations and representatives of FIFA.

Northern Irishmen are to be thanked for the introduction of two of the most important developments in the game: the penalty kick proposed by goalkeeper William McCrum and the offside rule proposed by Billy McCracken.

Until partition in 1921 the IFA governed football across the whole island of Ireland; thereafter the Football Association of Ireland (FAI) governed football in the Republic. Today the IFA is responsible for football in the six northern counties of Ulster: Antrim, Armagh, Down, Fermanagh, Londonderry and Tyrone.

The population of Northern Ireland is approximately 1.8 million and most of the players who represent their country at international level are playing at club level across the water in England and Scotland. Only a handful of the senior internationals play in the English Premiership, with most plying their trade in the Championship.

I enjoyed a very privileged position working in Northern Ireland; first of all liaising directly with IFA chief executive Howard Wells and latterly on a personal basis for Lawrie Sanchez. Both these roles meant I was privy to many confidential meetings, experiences and conversations. In both of these positions I was working as a communications consultant not as an investigative journalist and I have not betrayed the confidences with which I was entrusted.

All quotes in this book are taken from interviews conducted specifically for this book during June and early July 2007 before the completion of the UEFA Euro 2008 qualifying tournament and are given by the named sources with their full cooperation. All references to caps and clubs are accurate for those months. The opinions expressed by individuals are not necessarily my own.

When Lawrie Sanchez took over as manager of Northern Ireland he was not a universally popular choice. Recently sacked from Wycombe Wanderers in the Second Division of the English League and with previous managerial experience only at Sligo Rovers some considered him inexperienced. To make matters worse he wasn't even Northern Irish.

But on the other side of the coin, the job on offer didn't appear terribly attractive either. The team were floating slowly towards oblivion. Ranked 124th in the world by FIFA, without a win in 13 games and with the last goal scored over two years previously there wasn't a lot to shout about. At his first press conference Lawrie stated he would do three things: start scoring; start winning; and move up the rankings. Who could have predicted success would come so rapidly and spectacularly?

With a squad consisting of more or less the same players who had achieved so little, Lawrie turned things around and created the headline grabbing Team Northern Ireland who made the world sit up and take notice.

This book is a celebration of those years.

1 LAWRIE'S ARRIVAL AS NORTHERN IRELAND MANAGER

Lawrie Sanchez has a habit of causing major upsets against all the odds. In management and as a player he has scored victories in the most unexpected situations.

In his playing career with Wimbledon he scored the promotion-winning goal that took the London club out of the old Second Division and into the top tier; as well as scoring the winner in Wimbledon's FA Cup-winning clash over Liverpool in 1988.

Moving into management as player/manager with Sligo Rovers in 1994 he stayed for a year before returning to Wimbledon for several years as reserve team manager and first team coach.

In February 1999 Lawrie joined Wycombe Wanderers in the English Second Division helping them to avoid relegation and leading the club to an FA Cup semi-final in 2001 against his old adversary Liverpool. In September 2003 Lawrie was sacked by Wycombe but his greater victories were just around the corner …

LAWRIE SANCHEZ:

"I'm a great believer in circles, life is full of circles.

"I began my playing career at Reading at the age of 17 and my first match was against Wimbledon with Dave Bassett in the centre of midfield. He later became my manager when I played at Wimbledon. Then my last full game as a professional player in England was for Swindon against Wimbledon.

"When I took over at Wycombe we were fighting relegation. Towards the end of the season we had a match against

Macclesfield, who were managed by Sammy McIlroy. We beat them, we avoided relegation, they got relegated. The following Christmas Sammy took over as manager of Northern Ireland and at that time I thought, as you have to do as a manager, where is my next job? And I thought of Sammy at Northern Ireland and thought perhaps that was a job I could do.

"So lo and behold four years later I get the sack from Wycombe on 30 September 2003.

"About two weeks later Sammy McIlroy walks out of Northern Ireland and takes over at Stockport. And I'm thinking someone is trying to tell me something."

Stephen Alexander from Ballymena, County Antrim, has supported Northern Ireland all his life. Although he is a journalist he has never worked at the matches. "I go there as a fan," he states. "I have never worked at a Northern Ireland match, written a match report or gone to the post-match press conference. I am a supporter." He is a block booker in the North Stand.

STEPHEN ALEXANDER:

"Windsor Park, in the days before Lawrie's Northern Ireland were playing, was half empty.

"Obviously there were things going on at that time with accusations of sectarian chanting and generally speaking it wasn't a good time to be a Northern Ireland fan. The team were trawling the depths on the field. The reputation of the fans was not the best in the eyes of the footballing world. Generally speaking it had become a bind, a hassle, to go to Northern Ireland matches and it

would be accurate in my case to say that I wasn't sure about renewing my block booking. It was that bad. Northern Ireland supporters are renowned for their loyalty but I think there are limits to what people can take.

"We had gone for 13 matches without a win and also failed to score. It was absolutely depressing. I was just thinking, let's get to the end of this campaign and I'll decide what to do next. And then the manager stepped down. I was fairly happy to see him go. I had nothing against the man personally; he had been a very good player for Northern Ireland. He had also proved himself in club management in the lower divisions; I just felt that he was a bit out of his depth tactically at international level.

"Very few people wore the Northern Ireland shirt on the streets. That may have been partly due to sectarian issues but I think it was more that you would have been laughed at in the street. I know that sounds ridiculous but only the most passionate, loyal supporters would have worn a Northern Ireland shirt in the street at that stage.

"To the general public who just looked at results they saw a team who hadn't scored for 13 matches. It was almost the embarrassment factor. The only time you would see people in Northern Ireland shirts was at the matches."

LAWRIE SANCHEZ:

"I phoned the Irish Football Association (IFA) and asked what they were doing about the job vacancy and they said there was no rush to appoint a new manager because the draw for the World Cup qualifiers wasn't for some time, but they wanted someone with Northern Ireland qualifications, so I knew I qualified. I told the general secretary David Bowen I was very interested and what should I do? He said they noted my interest but they didn't want to do anything for a couple of months. So I asked: 'Do I hang on hoping I'll get a chance and get on the shortlist or do I just apply for other jobs?' And I think David said I would have a chance and would certainly be on the shortlist so I said I would hang on because that's what I was interested in.

"So I took a gamble and every month I phoned up and said,

'What are you going to do? When are you going to appoint?' and they said there was no rush because there wasn't a competitive game until February.

"The draw for the World Cup was done in December and England and Wales were in the group and I thought, 'Awh that knocks my chances,' because obviously there's going to be one or two big name candidates who are out of work who are going to be interested. So I phoned up again and said, 'What's happening now there's been the World Cup draw?' and David said nothing had changed, they were still looking for people with Northern Ireland credentials and they would be discussing candidates over the next few weeks."

NI FAN STEPHEN ALEXANDER:

"I was excited when the World Cup draw was made because I'd been watching Northern Ireland for ten, twelve years and they had never played England in that time. I was tremendously excited, and also with Wales, but I remember thinking it was a really, really difficult group. I remember thinking, can we avoid finishing bottom of that group? Azerbaijan were the supposedly lowest ranked team in the group. That's how low it was, you were actually thinking can we beat the lowest ranked team in our group? That's the level of self-doubt that had crept in at that stage."

LAWRIE SANCHEZ:

"I got a phone call from the IFA in January and they said they'd like to interview me. I went over to Belfast, to Windsor Avenue and it was the first time I had been there because as a player, when I played for Northern Ireland, you never went to Windsor Avenue. It's a lovely old building, I was aware it was the former home of Thomas Andrews, the designer of the Titanic, and I thought there was a certain irony there because of the position the team was in at the time.

"I got picked up from the airport by William Campbell (IFA Head of Finance and Personnel at the time) and he took me to the Stormont Hotel and I said, 'What are we doing here?' and he said they were still interviewing another candidate and they wanted to keep us apart. So I was kept in a holding station. I later found it was Jimmy Nicholl, he was the favourite for the job, he had so many caps playing for Northern Ireland and was a World Cup legend. But I went along, there were a lot of people on the interview panel, the president Jim Boyce, general secretary David Bowen, vice president Raymond Kennedy, William Campbell and members of the international committee.

"I outlined my points but I think the thing which swung it was when they asked who my assistant manager would be and I said Gerry Armstrong had agreed to do the job. All ears pricked up, Gerry was part of the World Cup squad and they felt that if someone of his calibre wanted to work with me as my assistant it would be easier to sell to the Northern Ireland fans.

"I knew Gerry through our time in football and had called to ask him if he would work with me and when I got the job he asked, 'How did you pull that one off?' And I said, 'Look Gerry we're going to try and pull a few things off now.' The first person I met when I went to Windsor Avenue for my interview was Derek McKinley, who had been the kit man during my playing days and was still there in that role. It was nice to see a familiar face and he welcomed me. Jimmy Nicholl was still in the building and I went across to say hello to him."

David Bowen was general secretary of the IFA for 21 years and sat on the interview panel that selected Lawrie as manager.

DAVID BOWEN:

"I knew Lawrie when he played for Northern Ireland and I spoke to him once or twice after his three games. He was quite hurt at the end of the day that he wasn't selected again. Billy Bingham, the manager at that time, didn't select him for whatever reasons. I wasn't privy to that.

"Lawrie rang me a couple of times to ask what I thought the problem was and I said I wasn't aware of any problem it was purely Billy's selection.

"Lawrie had an excellent interview for the manager's job.

There were only the two candidates considered and he had an excellent interview. He impressed the international committee with his knowledge of the game and his ideas and forthright opinions on how Northern Ireland could progress. For a number of reasons and circumstances we ended up offering him the job."

Jim Boyce was president of the IFA at the time of Lawrie's interview and throughout his years as manager.

JIM BOYCE:

"Lawrie's personality, commitment and tactical awareness convinced people that he could turn the fortunes of Northern Ireland around, which of course he then went on to do."

NI FAN STEPHEN ALEXANDER:

"The two names in the frame were Lawrie Sanchez and Jimmy Nicholl, who had been in for the job before when Sammy McIlroy got it. I have to say I wasn't overly excited by the prospect of either of them but I do remember thinking Jimmy Nicholl had been overlooked the previous time so I thought he was a near certainty to get it on this occasion.

"I was aware of Lawrie from his playing days, obviously he scored the winning goal for Wimbledon in the FA Cup final, that had made him a well-known name in football. And then he had been working away as a club manager, working quietly behind the scenes at Wycombe Wanderers and took them to the semi-finals of the FA Cup and that catapulted Wycombe and Lawrie into the spotlight. I think everyone in Northern Ireland was aware of him, he'd won a couple of caps [three] for Northern Ireland as a player but certainly you couldn't say he had a distinguished international career in the same way as someone like Sammy McIlroy or Jimmy Nicholl had. I was convinced Jimmy Nicholl would get the job."

The IFA and Jimmy Nicholl, who was with Scottish club Dunfermline at the time, could not agree personal terms and so the job was offered to Lawrie.

NI FAN STEPHEN ALEXANDER:

"I was really stunned the day I heard the announcement that Lawrie had got the job, I was flabbergasted. I think that was the general feeling with all the fans. I know it sounds daft, with Lawrie having been a Northern Ireland international, but he was one of the players brought in through the parents or grandparents rule and Lawrie himself didn't have any particular association with the country of Northern Ireland. Lawrie was considered almost an Englishman because he had played his entire career there and lived there.

"I think most fans thought the IFA would go down that road again of employing a Northern Irishman."

LAWRIE SANCHEZ:

"I flew over for the press conference at Windsor Avenue. The IFA told me they had never seen anything like it, there was so much media interest, not just within Northern Ireland but SKY television was there as well. Up until then Northern Ireland hadn't been considered such a big story. They were very surprised, but it was an indication of what was to come.

"I wondered what I should say. At my interview for the job I had indicated that my aims were to get Northern Ireland scoring again, get them winning and rise up the FIFA rankings. Everyone needs something to hang their hat on and I had thought, 'What do Northern Ireland need to succeed?' And it was quite obvious what they needed, I just had to express it. And so I did, at my interview and at the press conference."

The IFA's press officer John Quinn had retired in December 2003 and not been replaced. His student placement assistant Denise Ward, 23 at the time, was looking after media matters.

DENISE WARD:

"Just coming back from our Christmas break in January 2004 there was so much speculation as to who was going to be the new Northern Ireland manager. According to the media, Lawrie was an outsider in the list of people being interviewed by the IFA and to be honest I had never ever heard of him, but maybe this was down to the fact I am a girl and had never previously followed Northern Ireland.

"I worked in the IFA press office during all this, I was also a full-time student doing Business Studies at the University of Ulster. And during the time of the new manager's appointment I was admittedly out of my depth as the media interest was intense. But under the management of the IFA at that time PR and a strong positive media relationship were not high up on their list, if on the list at all.

"Once the new manager was decided, I wasn't told who it would be, I was simply told to give David Currie (IFA Head of International Administration) my contact lists for the media to be invited to a press conference on 22 January 2004. The press conference was downstairs in the Trophy Room at Windsor Avenue before a huge media presence and a large representation of the IFA committee.

"Nobody could move at this conference such was the volume of people interested in this new appointment, I was stood at the IFA reception handing out a press release and chatting with other staff – some of us jested that we should have put money on Lawrie becoming the manager because he was such an outsider we would have made money.

"When Lawrie stepped into this post he inherited a severe goal drought left by previous manager Sammy Mac [sic]. I hate to add the cliché but things could only get better. Lawrie set himself three main aims and he very quickly started to tick all of those aims off his list."

Mark McIntosh, from Lisburn, County Antrim is a freelance football writer working primarily for the *Sunday Mirror*. He has covered Northern Ireland internationals for ten years.

MARK McINTOSH:

"Following Northern Ireland under Sammy McIlroy wasn't as depressing as some people might think. Our fans were exactly the

ABOVE: Northern Ireland journalist, Mark McIntosh.

ABOVE: Not long after his appointment as Northern Ireland manager, Lawrie attended a fund-raising dinner organised by the Amalgamation of Northern Ireland Supporters' Clubs in aid of local charity Heartbeat. Lawrie bid for the shirt worn by World Cup legend Billy Cunningham when he played in the 1958 World Cup finals in Sweden. Here he is pictured with Billy and the shirt.

same then as they are now, the only thing different is that there are a lot more now. It was almost typical Northern Ireland gallows humour. Even when we couldn't score goals we were singing. The atmosphere, although it is louder now, was very similar.

"The press box was pretty similar. We all had a bit of craic it was just quieter because, when we didn't get results, boring wouldn't be the word, but it was the same old thing every time whereas when Lawrie took over it was, 'Well what's gonna happen now?' Because there was always something.

"I was at his first press conference. It was absolutely full. I think that was to do with the World Cup draw because nobody was expecting Lawrie to get the job. Initially I think people were going more to ask questions of the IFA rather than Lawrie Sanchez but the difference came within five minutes of him opening his mouth. He said all the right things. He had people eating out of his hand. Whether it would last or not we felt he had certainly played a blinder so far. He set himself certain targets, the first was to score a goal, then he wanted to win a match and wanted to climb the rankings. He said that from the outset.

"Afterwards myself and a few others in the media brought

Lawrie down to Windsor Park to get some pictures of him in the centre circle. That was very laid back and he was chatting about things other than football. He had us eating out of the palm of his hands, he said all the things that people wanted to hear. That's what the IFA said at the time, they said his interview was incredible."

2 FIRST GOAL AND FIRST WIN

As well as Northern Ireland legend Gerry Armstrong, Lawrie's backroom team included two of his former Wimbledon team mates, Terry Gibson and Dave Beasant.

Diminutive Terry is the kind of guy who brings a smile to everyone's face because a smile is always planted on his own. His playing career started at Manchester United and took in Tottenham as well as the Wimbledon Crazy Gang. When Lawrie managed Wycombe, Terry worked alongside him as coach and it was a job he was asked to replicate with Northern Ireland.

TERRY GIBSON:

"After Lawrie left Wycombe it all became a bit messy and I had to bide my time until things resolved themselves. Lawrie wanted me to work with him at Northern Ireland and Wycombe wouldn't allow it at first but it all got resolved in the end and I was there to work with Lawrie for the first match against Norway in February.

"Lawrie is a strong character but looking back now he knows he stayed too long at Wycombe. There were a number of things that happened at the club towards the end of his reign; the wage bill was cut drastically and there was a wage deferral scheme amongst the players and staff and that really did cut into the squad. We had to release a lot of experienced players and replace

OPPOSITE: The first team photograph under Lawrie's management, Northern Ireland v Norway at Windsor Park in Belfast when David Healy broke the 1,298-minute goal drought and scored.

them with youngsters. Before the season started we knew it was going to be an uphill struggle and I think Lawrie was hurt by the fact that two years previously to that he'd taken the club to the FA Cup semi-final and he felt he deserved a bit more loyalty from the people at Wycombe. Unfortunately that didn't come and I personally feel Lawrie was made the scapegoat for the politics at the club at the time.

"Lawrie told me about his Northern Ireland interview and said he felt he was the clear second favourite after Jimmy Nicholl, and the next thing I knew he'd got the job. It didn't surprise me, he creates a good impression at job interviews, he's very organised.

"He was very excited to become a national team manager which was totally different to what we'd been used to at Wycombe. He was just pleased to be back working full-time in football again, because for Lawrie it was a full-time job. The fact that it was a national team manager was a bonus.

"The main difference between club and international football was that it took three or four matches for us all, the players and backroom staff, to get to know each other. It probably wasn't until we went to the Caribbean in June that we all became a tight-knit group with trust between us. It wouldn't take that length of time at club level because you are together every day."

Sammy McIlroy was loved in Northern Ireland, he captained the 1986 World Cup team, had 88 caps and a buoyant personality. He was a popular choice to succeed Lawrie McMenemy in 2000 and in his first game in charge a young David Healy scored twice.

Ultimately however, his international managerial career was filled with frustration, not helped by player withdrawals and retirements, sectarian booing of Celtic's Neil Lennon and off-field incidents.

NI CAPTAIN AARON HUGHES:

"I felt with Sammy that he put everything into the job but there were certain times when the luck just wasn't with us. Sometimes you were putting in good performances and not getting the results. It was a hard time because no matter what we seemed to do it just didn't work out for us, but it certainly wasn't for lack of effort. Sammy was probably as gutted as we were when we came off the pitch having put everything into it and got nothing. He wasn't the kind of manager who could hide his feelings, you could see it.

"It didn't bother me at all that Lawrie was an Englishman. As much as it's nice to see someone from your country taking the job, for me it's about getting results. As long as he showed the same commitment as Sammy did and put everything into the job and made the players better.

"Straight away you could get a sense that it wasn't just a job for Lawrie, that he wouldn't just use it to step up to something bigger, he was here and he wanted to do it properly. He told the players, 'If you don't want to be here you don't have to be here. I just want the guys who want to be here and do well. And I don't want a Northern Ireland who are always used to being the underdogs, thinking if we don't win it's no big deal. I wanna change Northern Ireland football, I wanna take this team up the rankings.'"

LAWRIE SANCHEZ:

"Towards the end of Sammy's management he had been trying not to get beaten and so he played with a five-man midfield. The results show how good they were defensively with only eight goals conceded in eight games. That's not a bad average. The trouble is, playing so defensively with a five-man midfield and one striker up front you're never likely to score. So the run of games without a goal was not so surprising.

"In our first game against Norway we put David [Healy] up front with a big man, Andy Smith, alongside him."

NI SUPPORTER STEPHEN ALEXANDER:

"Lawrie inherited most of the same squad that Sammy had before him so that does underline the impact that Lawrie had on the team."

18 FEBRUARY 2004 – INTERNATIONAL FRIENDLY MATCH
NORTHERN IRELAND v NORWAY
WINDSOR PARK, BELFAST
RESULT: LOST 4–1
(DAVID HEALY)
ATTENDANCE: 11,288

NI COACH TERRY GIBSON:

"Lawrie has strong organisational skills and he made sure the players were aware of the style of play he wanted and of their responsibility in the team. It was quite simple really, everyone knew their job. Over a period of time the players just got better and better.

"When we first started out we had a 4–1 defeat at home to Norway, we could never have imagined then that within a couple of years we'd beat England, Spain and Sweden.

"I was amazed that Windsor Park was a sell-out, because the team had gone for 13 games without a goal and although it was quite a prestigious game against Norway it wasn't as if it was England or Brazil. It was the first time it had been a sell-out for a while and the fans really got behind us. The be all and end all of that game was to score a goal, the result was really immaterial. It came but we did concede within two minutes of scoring, such was the euphoria of everybody: the players, us, the supporters. But it was marvellous to get that first goal, it had to be David [Healy] who got it. He needed to get that monkey off his back, he'd had so many games without a goal and the record was going on and on

ABOVE: Patriotic David Healy got back to winning ways under Lawrie, scoring in the first match against Norway and netting the goal that won the game against Estonia.

and on. I don't think the players were particularly ecstatic about scoring that one goal, it was more relief. They weren't celebrating after the game, there was huge disappointment that we'd lost, but there was a resigned feeling that at least we'd scored. There was a quiet determination about them."

David Healy first played for Northern Ireland under Sammy McIlroy, and proved his loyalty to his country by turning up for almost every game during the two-year, 1,298-minute goal drought. When, finally, he found the net again during Lawrie's first game in charge it was a highly emotional moment for everyone.

DAVID HEALY:

"I think it was one of the biggest roars I have ever heard in Windsor Park, even though we were getting beat.

"Sammy was my first manager, playing against Luxembourg. There were occasions Sammy felt we had to play a 4–5–1 formation. Sometimes I played on my own up front and sometimes I played on the right of the five, it didn't always play to my strengths and Lawrie came in and had seen the games and probably saw why we weren't scoring or creating chances. It was the first thing he did when he came in, he said he wanted to get balls in the box not just when strikers were in the box, but between wide players to give everybody more opportunity. And for whatever reason I started scoring goals."

FORMER IFA PRESS OFFICER DENISE WARD:

"The Norway match at Windsor was Lawrie's first chance to break the goalless run. Although Northern Ireland got beaten 4–1 at Windsor that cold February night, Lawrie had set out what he

wanted to do and David Healy, with Preston at the time, scored. There was an air of excitement and anticipation in the press box, an increased media presence due to Lawrie's appointment.

"The first three Norway goals had gone in and the media were writing the next day's headlines, then David Healy scored from a header. Aim number one was accomplished and the media headlines turned from crucifying Northern Ireland to becoming less harsh and more optimistic for the road ahead. They could no longer harp on about this goal drought – thank God it was over.

"I was so pleased we scored, as it was my first goal experience. At the press conference Lawrie was very hopeful, he didn't let the scoreline affect him too much, after all he had set out what he wanted to do and no one could take that away or say anything different.

"He was getting to grips with what he had to work with and he just needed to get the players' confidence up and mould his side. Everyone was optimistic for the future."

NI JOURNALIST MARK McINTOSH:

"At the press conference after the match a few of us were still a little happy that we had scored and Lawrie said, 'We lost 4–1, I'm not happy about scoring a goal.' And everybody thought, 'Well this guy actually does mean business. Fair play.'

"He was showing that disciplinarian side straight away, yes we scored but we had conceded more than we had scored."

NI FAN STEPHEN ALEXANDER:

"There was a tremendous outpouring of relief. There was a good attendance; the fans had decided they were going to give Lawrie a chance. It wasn't all that encouraging a start in terms of the result, but if you were going to pick out one moment from that match it was that as we were going away from Windsor Park that night all we were talking about was the fact that we had seen Northern Ireland score and that was progress."

31 MARCH 2004 – INTERNATIONAL FRIENDLY MATCH
ESTONIA v NORTHERN IRELAND
LE COQ ARENA, TALLINN
RESULT: WON 1–0
(DAVID HEALY)
ATTENDANCE: 2,000

NI COACH TERRY GIBSON:

"A lot of players dropped out for this game, so there was a lot of calling around at the last minute. They had injuries and club commitments. We had a shadow squad, but it was indicative of the time that we had with the squad, that although we had players missing they were fantastic and we got that first win.

"Lawrie's strength is his meticulous planning and he puts things in place for all his staff. But I was surprised at how quickly things turned around. But when you look at the players we had, and their attitude, determination and enthusiasm I think they were just waiting for someone to come along and point them in the right direction and we were grateful that they were so eager to respond. It was a fantastic adventure."

DAVID HEALY:

"We were all very hopeful, but I was probably more hopeful than most that we were going to take off as I played in almost every one of those games where we didn't score. It was Estonia, not anybody high in the rankings, but it was great just to be winning again."

NI JOURNALIST MARK McINTOSH:

"After the match Lawrie was happy but he was saying, 'This is a friendly and it's great that we've got a bit of confidence and that's going to help us, but at the end of the day when the hard work

starts with the qualifiers that's when we've got to do this.' There was no bigging himself up.

"Little things were happening and you started to feel this guy could have a bit of luck on his side. I remember at his first press conference he told us he would rather be a lucky general than a great general and so it proved."

FORMER IFA GENERAL SECRETARY DAVID BOWEN:

"I was in Estonia and saw the victory. To win away from home was a big plus, the feel good factor, which increased with the wonderful results still to come, was beginning to progress.

"The appointment of Lawrie wasn't mine as such. I was certainly impressed and very much in favour of Lawrie. but the appointment was the international committee's, as indeed today it would be the executive committee's. I was in no doubt it was an excellent selection and therefore I was very much in favour of the appointment.

"I certainly did not anticipate the victories which happened against England, Spain and Sweden. I didn't think the turnaround would be as quick and as remarkable.

"It has to come down to the manager and players. At the end of the day it's the manager's job to get the best out of the players and Lawrie Sanchez succeeded in getting the best out of the squad."

NI FAN STEPHEN ALEXANDER:

"I wasn't there, but was aware of the result and delighted. I thought, 'Okay that's good, in his first match we scored the first goal in God knows how long, in his second match we managed to win a game. Maybe this fella has something about him.'"

Big Dave Beasant, who stands 6 feet 4 inches tall, has known Lawrie for years. They roomed together during their playing career at Wimbledon, did their coaching badges together and always hoped they could work with one another in the future. After his playing career was over, Dave secured a job as goalkeeping coach with English Premiership club Fulham.

28 APRIL 2004 – INTERNATIONAL FRIENDLY MATCH
NORTHERN IRELAND v SERBIA AND MONTENEGRO
WINDSOR PARK, BELFAST
RESULT: DRAW 1–1
(JAMES QUINN)
ATTENDANCE: 9,690

DAVE BEASANT:

"I was driving to training at Fulham when I heard the news on the radio about Lawrie's appointment with Northern Ireland. I rang him straight away to offer congratulations and in the conversation he said he was going to try and get me involved. He wanted to get the set-up right.

"I was in full-time employment with Fulham so I had to get permission from the club and manager Chris Coleman. My two main goalkeepers at Fulham were internationals and away during international weeks themselves so it was not a major issue for me to be away.

"Lawrie and I knew that we would work well together and have a good relationship. We're not totally the same people, we have similar ideas but as far as personalities and characters go we're quite different, but once you've been with someone for so long you understand how they work. A lot of people who don't know Lawrie think he's dour and he's not, he's just got a different sense of humour, a very dry sense of humour and you have to know the man to understand him.

"It was quite a jump for me to go from not being a coach, to being a Premiership coach and then an international coach. But as soon as Lawrie asked me I wanted to do it. You want to test yourself and try at the highest level. I was very lucky.

"Whenever Lawrie speaks to a group of players he makes me listen. I listen to what he says because he says the right things and I'm listening thinking, 'Well yeah he's right, we can do this.' Lawrie

ABOVE: Northern Ireland goalkeeping coach, Dave Beasant, with Northern Ireland coach, Terry Gibson.

started to instil belief and confidence, saying on paper we might not be as good as the individuals we are playing against but as a team we are all in it together.

"The way Lawrie decided he was going to play his football raised a few eyebrows with some thinking this is not how we play international football. Sanch said, 'You play international football to win games and you haven't been winning games with the way you have been playing, so if you do it the way I want I think you have a good chance of winning games.'

"Some people say that international football is played by passing the ball out the back, having 24 passes before you get over the halfway line and then you lose it to the other team and they have 24 passes and then hopefully you win it back and have some more passes. It's a slower game. When you play against teams who are not used to a different style you can progress because as soon as you get the ball you're putting them under pressure, you're hustling, you're playing as a team.

"Later on teams didn't like playing against Northern Ireland, they couldn't handle the work rate of the players. It was all down to the players. Once they bought the ticket of what Sanch was trying to do everyone starting believing it. That first goal against Norway, although we lost 4–1, scoring after 13 games without a goal the jubilation from the fans that night was as if we'd won the game. It was such a relief. That was just the beginning for David Healy.

"The reason why David hadn't been scoring goals was because he wasn't given the supply where he needed it. He needs the ball in the 18-yard box or somewhere around there because he scores some unbelievable goals from outside it. Him scoring that goal was the beginning of something special in Sanch's reign.

"The Serbia and Montenegro match saw James Quinn score. Quinney didn't have a prolific goal-scoring record and as the campaign went along Quinney was happy to play shotgun type of thing for David Healy, in fact David needed someone else to play alongside him as a bigger target man. But in this game against Serbia I can remember a move, I think it came from Bairdy [Chris Baird] down the line to David and this time it was David who did the work outside the box. Sometimes your best goal scorer can also be your best supplier as well. He got down the edge and crossed the ball into the six-yard box where Quinney put it in at the back post. For Dave to make the goal for Quinney proves that they complimented each other quite well.

"My biggest memory of being with Northern Ireland is of meeting up with such a great bunch of lads. The players came from such a wide spectrum of divisions, the Premier Division, the majority from the Championship and some from the Second Division and the Irish League like Andy Smith and Gary Hamilton. To get those boys all together, I used to enjoy meeting up with them because everyone had different stories to tell.

"We are very lucky with facilities in the Premier Division. I remember our first Northern Ireland training session before the Norway game, I can't remember the name of the ground but we only trained there for that one week. The portable goals were not portable, they were really heavy and needed about 15 people to carry them. When we lifted the goals up they started to creak and break, there weren't any markers, and there just wasn't the equipment. Lawrie said we had to find a better training facility and somewhere where we could use portable goals.

"We moved to Newforge where the facilities were brilliant in comparison to what we had before. The equipment just hadn't been there for an international set-up. Lawrie tried to rectify it and set standards. Players respond and respect the fact that you are trying to do the best for them. We were trying to create an environment where the players were happy."

James Quinn had played under three previous Northern Ireland managers before Lawrie arrived, but missed the first two games due to injury.

JAMES QUINN:

"Lawrie was my best Northern Ireland manager; his record says that, his achievements, the rankings say that, the position we're in at the minute [at time of writing, June 2007]. It's just one of those weird things, he got together a bunch of players that clicked. He organised us. For about six years we hadn't been organised, no one really knew their jobs. We turned up, we had a couple of five-a-sides and that was it, 'Go and play against Germany.' We were in no way organised enough to be able to play the best teams in the world.

"When Lawrie came in I was injured and playing in Holland so I could have been forgotten, there is no reason why he should coming looking for me, but he did. My first cap under Lawrie was against Serbia and Montenegro and I remember in the first training session I had under him he told us how to play. He started with me and David up front and he told us how it was gonna work. He told us, with respect, we were not going to outplay a lot of these teams. We had to do it through hard work, organisation and team spirit.

"Twenty-five minutes into the game the exact moves we had practiced in the training session repeated themselves. Chris Baird played the ball down to David Healy, David Healy crossed to me and I scored to the back post and I thought, 'Whoa!' We had practised those exact moves two days before. I was thinking, 'Hold on, he might have got something here.'

"The lads trusted him after that."

TRIP TO THE CARIBBEAN: THREE INTERNATIONAL FRIENDLY AWAY MATCHES

28 MAY 2004 –

v BARBADOS

DRAW 1-1

(DAVID HEALY)

2 JUNE 2004 –

v ST KITTS AND NEVIS

WON 2-0

(DAVID HEALY, STEVE JONES)

6 JUNE 2004 –

v TRINIDAD AND TOBAGO

WON 3-0

(DAVID HEALY X 2, STUART ELLIOTT)

Suddenly, David Healy just couldn't stop scoring. After netting one in each of Lawrie's first two games he now grabbed a further four on a tour of the Caribbean which had been arranged before Lawrie's appointment.

NI COACH TERRY GIBSON:

"The training facilities and the pitches that we played on weren't what we expected. It took some getting used to for the players. Our first match was in Barbados and that was a poor pitch and it got even worse in St Kitts.

"One or two of the players had been a bit disillusioned in Barbados and we assured them it would be better in St Kitts and when we got there it was even worse. We walked into the stadium to see the pitch we would be training on, which was to be the same pitch we played on, and there were goats on the pitch, just roaming around, that's the way it was in St Kitts.

"When we got to Tobago the pitch at the Dwight Yorke Stadium was fabulous, first rate. So that was a bonus for us because we kept assuring the players things would get better.

"It was good to get the players together for a ten-day period. At the end of the first season it was a real plus for us. From a football point of view we did really well.

"I also remember the Caribbean tour for Jeff Whitley's attitude at that time. He'd played for Sunderland in the play-off semi-finals and Jeff had missed the penalty in the penalty shoot-out that would have taken them to the final. Jeff actually made his own way out because we were already in the Caribbean, I think he must have had about six different flights, he'd been travelling near enough for 24 hours, it was so ridiculous to get to St Kitt's from where he was. And I remember him turning up and we were all on the beach and he said he felt awful because he'd spent all this time alone on the plane thinking about the penalty that he had missed for Sunderland that cost them a place in the play-off final and the chance to get into the Premiership. The amount of stick and abuse he got for missing that penalty, it was affectionate but it was typical football banter and Jeff said to me he couldn't believe the stick he got, he'd expected them to put their arms around him and feel sorry for him. But they just took the mickey but it was affectionate and it made Jeff feel at home straight away and from then on he said he could put it to the back of his mind and the last thing he had wanted was for them to feel sorry for him.

"He had travelled all on his own after that heartbreak and made his own way to the Caribbean and I think that summed Jeff up at that time to be honest. He wanted to be involved in international football, so it was a big surprise when eventually he did what he did prior to the England game and never made the attempt to get back in the squad."

NI JOURNALIST MARK McINTOSH:

"We drew one match and won two games. Nobody could believe what was happening. The first match was a bit strange, the referee and linesmen were awful and the players were probably still a bit tired, but we drew with Barbados. And then with St Kitts we won and there was a little bit of, okay we knew we were a better team than who we were playing but it was still massive and then everybody started talking about David Healy and could he break

Colin Clarke and Billy Gillespie's Northern Ireland goal-scoring record in the Caribbean? Then to go to Trinidad and Tobago, who were certainly a better side than us, and to beat them, and Healy scored twice that night and broke the record which had stood at 13 goals.

"The match was played at the Dwight Yorke Stadium in Bacolet and they had an Olympic sprinter running around the side of the pitch on an athletics track with the Trinidad and Tobago flag and then one of our fans jumped over a wall with a Northern Ireland flag and decided to chase him.

"It was very light hearted and when he finally caught up with him he was sprinting and the other guy was walking and they put their arms around each other and ran around with both flags."

FORMER IFA PRESS OFFICER DENISE WARD:

"I wasn't sent with the squad to the Caribbean, I had just graduated and it was considered too big a job for me. Only a handful of media went. But the World Cup qualifiers were coming up next and if I was expected to do all the media travel arrangements and press passes I wanted to go on the trips too: my job didn't end in Belfast. On a trip there were press conferences, media requests and interviews to be done in the host country and I felt I should be allowed to do this."

William Cherry has been a professional photographer for over 20 years and supplied many of the pictures displayed in this book. Now working with Presseye in Belfast he has covered the Northern Ireland home games since 1989 and the away games since 1995.

WILLIAM CHERRY:

"My wife Toni was 32 weeks pregnant when the team travelled to the Caribbean. Toni and I talked about whether or not I should make the trip, but we thought everything would be fine since there was nearly another two months before she was due. Sure enough, her waters broke on my first full day in Barbados. I got a call in the early hours of the morning, and was told there was no indication

that she was actually in labour but after talking to the team doctor for advice, I decided to go home and spent ten hours waiting for a flight. Our daughter Katie Jean was born while I was pacing in the airport in Barbados – she was seven weeks early and weighed just 4lbs 10oz, but at least she was healthy. Through the entire ordeal, I have to say the team and staff were so supportive."

18 AUGUST 2004 – INTERNATIONAL FRIENDLY MATCH
SWITZERLAND v NORTHERN IRELAND
HARDTURM STADIUM, ZURICH
RESULT: DRAW 0–0
ATTENDANCE: 4,000

NI COACH TERRY GIBSON:

"The most difficult period of Lawrie's reign I think was the first year because the players had gone a long time without scoring a goal or getting a win and all of a sudden Lawrie, Dave and I turn up and you have to earn the trust and respect of the players. The players we had at the beginning, we've still got some left, there's Aaron (Hughes), Maik Taylor, Keith Gillespie, David Healy, Damien Johnson, Stephen Craigan but along the way we shouldn't forget the contribution of people like Mark Williams, Jeff Whitley, Danny Sonner and Colin Murdock.

"They were fantastic and invaluable in the first year when it wasn't glamorous to turn up and play for Northern Ireland, they gave their all when we were trying to set something in motion. They are all fantastic characters and they brought a lot to the squad in terms of personality and ability. Even after they had fallen out of the squad, we used to sit in hotels and tell stories with fondness about them all and I hope they appreciate what we felt about them because we couldn't have beaten England and Spain and Sweden without the contribution they made in that first year or two."

3 WORLD CUP QUALIFYING GAMES
POLAND AND WALES

The games everyone had been waiting for now started. But after a superb run of friendly draws and wins the first match that actually mattered, the opener in the World Cup qualifiers, was lost in a 3–0 thrashing at Windsor Park.

4 SEPTEMBER 2004 – FIFA WORLD CUP 2006 QUALIFYING ROUNDS

NORTHERN IRELAND v POLAND

WINDSOR PARK, BELFAST

RESULT: LOST 3–0

ATTENDANCE: 12,487

LAWRIE SANCHEZ:

"We went into the Poland game on the back of a six game undefeated run. Having lost to Norway we'd then gone six games, including the Caribbean tour, without losing a game. Everybody was starting to get a bit carried away I thought, about how good we were and how well everything was going and that Poland would come to town in the first game of the World Cup campaign and we'd knock them over. This, considering we hadn't won in the eight qualifying games in the previous campaign and hadn't scored a goal.

"I knew Poland were a good team, and the fact is by the end of the tournament most of the prominent Polish players were playing in either the Premiership or the Championship in decent sides which was an indication of how good they were.

"We lost 3–0. We came out and froze and fully deserved to get beaten 3–0, could possibly have been more, and it was a massive anti-climax after everything that had gone on before.

"If you count the Iceland game [Euro 2008], in four out of the five most recent qualifying campaigns we lost the opening game 3–0. Strange as it was, perhaps it wasn't so strange. And Poland were good, they were a better team than they were given credit for by an awful lot of people. I knew that.

"I was devastated, the players were devastated. There was massive expectation, sold-out games at home all of a sudden. People just expected us to turn up and roll over Poland.

"The very fact that it had rained all week prior to the game and we had trained in rain and then the morning of the game the sun came out set me ill at ease. I thought, 'I don't need the sun shining down on the team on a Saturday afternoon.' We needed to be hard working and work our socks off.

"When the sun comes out it sometimes takes the edge off the ability to work hard. If you're in rain or poor weather or it's night it's easier to work than when the sun's shining on you and everyone's in tee shirts watching the game.

"Having trained all week in the rain I thought, 'Great it's going to be pouring tomorrow, Windsor crowd behind us, all the good stuff going on.' Then I woke up and saw the sun out and I thought, 'This is going to be difficult today it's not going to go the way everyone is expecting,' and it ultimately didn't.

"Everybody was shocked, but I wasn't quite as shocked as everybody else. Poland were good, England had to beat them in the *last game to qualify above them. In hindsight we perhaps expected too much."*

Alan Ferris has supported the Northern Ireland football team practically all his life, first going to matches as a small boy in the 1960s with his father Geordie, and now taking his own son Johnny. Following the draw for the World Cup 2006 qualifiers, along with his brother and two friends, he formed the Bangor Northern Ireland Supporters Club. Alan is a block booker in Windsor Park's Kop Stand, home to the most fervent supporters who sing throughout every match, and he travels to many of the away games. He had been initially sceptical at the appointment of Lawrie but intrigued by reports that the new manager had arrived at his interview with a briefcase full of ideas. Alan was prepared to back Lawrie 100 per cent; he had witnessed the first goal against Norway; had travelled to the freezing cold of Tallin in Estonia to celebrate the first win; and had enjoyed a companionable trip to Zurich with the Green And White Army (GAWA) to see a spirited performance by the lads.

ALAN FERRIS:

"We began the 2006 campaign with renewed hope and anticipation. Fans of our wee country (OWC) are the eternal optimists. We lost to Poland, in my opinion, down to mistakes on the pitch, not mistakes on the bench. I was deflated, the thoughts were, 'Here we go again. We are out of the competition before it's even started.' All our hopes, dreams and unfulfilled promises were shattered. We trudged from Windsor Park downbeat, dreading the inevitable defeat at our next game."

NI JOURNALIST MARK McINTOSH:

"It was upsetting, but to be fair, before the games Lawrie was saying that we had to remember that we were playing sides that were better than us right now. And yes we'd gone to the Caribbean and done well and Switzerland went well but I think maybe a lot of people were still expecting it.

"I wasn't overly surprised that we lost to Poland, I was very surprised at how we lost. Every one of the goals was a ridiculous

mistake. I think there was slightly more pressure on the squad because they'd started to do a bit well and then as soon as they went one goal down that was it. They weren't used to being in that sort of position in the last two games, and they reverted back to type, they didn't know how to win."

NI SUPPORTER ALAN FERRIS:

"We were naturally deflated after the Poland defeat but travelled to Wales on the Tuesday with hope and optimism. It was my son's third away game. The build up began on the Tuesday, our plane from Belfast to Cardiff was full of the GAWA, the IFA president Jimmy Boyce was also on the plane, he sat and talked to the fans and opined that we would get a positive result. The streets of Cardiff were covered in green and white, all of the GAWA were in great form and eagerly awaiting the opportunity to visit one of the world's greatest stadia.

"My Dad and I attended a hotel on the Tuesday night and took part in a live radio interview which was jointly hosted by Radio Ulster and Radio Wales personalities. Jackie Fullerton was the front man for Northern Ireland and during this interview fans from both Northern Ireland and Wales spoke openly about their thoughts on the game and other football related matters.

"On the Wednesday morning a football match between the Northern Ireland and Welsh fans took place in Princess Gardens. This was part of a triangular tournament involving fans from Azerbaijan as well, the proceeds of which went to charity. This match had been advertised on the fans website www.ourweecountry.co.uk I had also plugged it during the radio interview on the previous night. Nearly 400 Northern Ireland fans turned up to cheer us on. SKY, BBC and UTV afforded us live media coverage. The opening moments of the game went out live on SKY Sports News during which time we scored our first goal. The goal scorer and the team were famous for five minutes! This set the tone for the rest of the day as we mingled with the Welsh fans in bars and clubs during the afternoon, then early evening we began our march to the Millennium Stadium.

"I had travelled with my dad and my son Johnny. Outside the stadium we met up with my uncle and two cousins who live in

England. One of my cousins had travelled from Hong Kong, the other had just returned from a tour of the Middle East with the Royal Navy. Although my cousins have English accents they cheered the Ulstermen on with the rest of the GAWA. That night was exceptional!"

Kate Hoey, Labour Member of Parliament for Vauxhall, south London, England since 1989 was born in County Antrim and attended Northern Ireland matches with her father from the age of ten, carrying a folding stool to stand on the terracing beneath the director's boxes. When she became the first female to be appointed Sports Minister in 1999, one of her first official engagements was to watch a Northern Ireland match. She tries never to miss a game and for several years now has been to every home and away fixture.

KATE HOEY MP:

"When I get the dates I just put them in my diary. I've missed the odd vote in the House of Commons, obviously nothing that was going to bring the government down. You just get that you really want to be there.

"The Welsh match was brilliant. I had come up from London and my train had been stopped for about 45 minutes because somebody jumped onto the line. I missed the first goal, as I was coming up the steps I heard a huge cheer and I just assumed that Wales must have scored. Of course when I got in I discovered that we'd scored."

ABOVE: Lawrie with his assistant manager, World Cup legend Gerry Armstrong, prior to kick-off at the Millennium Stadium, Cardiff.

8 SEPTEMBER 2004 – FIFA WORLD CUP 2006 QUALIFYING ROUNDS
WALES v NORTHERN IRELAND
MILLENNIUM STADIUM, CARDIFF
RESULT: DRAW 2–2
(JEFF WHITLEY, DAVID HEALY)
ATTENDANCE: 63,500

FORMER IFA PRESS OFFICER DENISE WARD:

"It was exhilarating when Northern Ireland were on form and scoring – I recall the match against Wales at a very impressive Millennium Stadium in Cardiff. The media facilities were top class, I was suitably embarrassed when it came to media facilities at Windsor. I remember coming out and looking at all the Northern Ireland fans before taking my seat. There was an electric charge to the atmosphere – Michael Hughes was first to go off in the first ten minutes for an apparent foul on Robbie Savage who retaliated and earned himself a red card too; Northern Ireland soldiered on and scored their first goal through Jeff Whitley with the next goal coming from David Healy who was then sent off for his goal celebration – what a turn of events before half time. Two men down, 2–0 down. Intense was not the word for it – my nerves couldn't take the pressure although I was there in a professional capacity to conduct the duty and responsibility of my post; I couldn't cope and went to hide in the Ladies. I'm sure given the chance a few of the men on the bench would have wanted to turn away and

not look too. The 2–0 lead was over when John Hartson scored before half time to make it 2–1 and even more unbearable for me to take. Wales equalised courtesy of Robert Earnshaw. It was level. The match ended with a rather boring score line, a draw that didn't reflect the passion and intensity of what had just happened and what everyone witnessed – aside from me stuck in the lav. Lawrie was so chuffed at the press conference but very grounded, focusing on the next matches. Onwards and upwards!

"The flip side to this of course was that things didn't always go so well, Northern Ireland was at the losing end too a few times. I remember one or two times before the post-match press conference of a losing game I would go to fetch Lawrie and find him in the small boot room in Windsor opposite the changing rooms on his own, quietly reflecting on what had just happened and staying out of the way of the media."

DAVID HEALY:

"That was the only time I've ever been sent off in my international career and it was hugely disappointing. I had quite a few family and friends in the crowd. It was a huge night in Cardiff, with thousands of Norn Ireland supporters there. Red and yellow cards were being thrown around, still to this day I don't know what I did wrong.

"I went into the dressing room and I was pretty upset with my emotions fired up. Michael Hughes was already in there, he had been sent off about ten minutes earlier and we had a chat. He couldn't understand why or how I'd been sent off but we talked about it and we watched the game on TV in the dressing room, kicking every ball and hugely disappointed when Wales got back. We deserved more than a draw."

NI JOURNALIST MARK McINTOSH:

"It was nuts. Without a doubt we should have won. The referee was shocking. We had a blatant foul in the second half on Tony Capaldi, but we weren't given it. It was just ridiculous.

"It was a very exciting game. The thing I remember about it was

that Stephen Watson from the BBC and I were sitting together and when Northern Ireland scored the first time Stephen and I jumped up to celebrate and for whatever reason the people sitting around the press box didn't like that and so we got told off by the stewards. I remember one of them saying if you do that again you'll get thrown out and then when David Healy scored and put us two up our entire line went nuts and the guy gave up because we were all celebrating.

"I remember Pat Sheehan from The Sun even celebrated when Healy scored. You know what Pat's like, a typical sort of cockney geezer, nobody could quite believe that we'd gone 2–0 up especially after what had happened the Saturday before."

LAWRIE SANCHEZ:

"In this campaign everyone remembers the England game, but the night of theatre for me was the night in Wales at the Millennium.

"Danny Sonner, a midfield player, had been in the initial Caribbean tour and was a great lad to have around. He couldn't make the Poland game and probably wouldn't have played anyway, but he's one of those characters, he's fantastic to have around, he's the centre of any joke whether it's against him or anybody else. He was at the centre of all the mischief that was going on at the time, good mischief if you want. Very, very confident in his own abilities, perhaps a little bit too confident. But he couldn't make the Poland game because he'd got a problem with his back through a bad night's sleep so we said, 'Join up with us in Wales.'

"So I said to the staff as we were flying out on the Sunday, the one good thing is Danny's gonna be meeting us in Wales and whereas all the players were low on the back of the Poland result what Danny will do is flaming slaughter everybody for their performance which is what was needed. We needed someone to bring some revelry into the group. The minute we walked into the hotel he started on the banter and it was the best thing that happened for us that week, those three days. Danny brought in a lightness that was needed.

"My recollections of that game are all about Danny. He wasn't in the team basically. We had 20-odd players with us and I had to have the chat in the afternoon with the ones who weren't going to be on the bench. I said, 'Look Danny, you're not playing,' and he was really put out and wanted to go home.

"I said, 'Look Danny, I'm not being funny, but you're not in this squad, we've got a game tonight, you don't wanna be driving back up the M5 to Birmingham and find out we've had one of the best wins that Northern Ireland's ever had. If you did that you would no longer be part of the party.'

"He was disappointed, I could understand that. Having lost 3–0 to Poland, he was a midfield player and thought he might have a chance of playing. He'd been involved in our first win against Estonia and been on the Caribbean tour and taken part in the games we won.

"I told him that if he went home I wouldn't be able to pick him again ever and he wouldn't wanna be at home when we were beating Wales at the Millennium and he would miss out on the night and put an end to his international career.

"And he stayed and I saw him after the game in the dressing room and he came over and said, 'Well done gaffer' and said he would have been gutted not to have been there missing a game like that. And that was good.

"Danny is my memory of that game. Obviously there's all the stuff about David being sent off. But Danny was one of the unsung heroes who was involved in the Estonia game, not involved in the Wales game, but his banter lifted the boys up for that trip. That for me is the abiding memory.

"You've gotta remember Keith [Gillespie] wasn't involved in that game either. He was in the squad but didn't play. He didn't play against Poland either. Keith wasn't wanting to do what I wanted to do, to be honest. He was fighting it a little bit."

NI SUPPORTER ALAN FERRIS:

"The belief within the ranks of the GAWA was rising, Lawrie was beginning to win the hearts and minds of the most vocal supporters in the Kop Stand, he was our new leader."

ABOVE: Northern Ireland kit man Derek McKinley.

Lawrie's backroom team included three Belfast-based personnel whom he inherited from previous regimes: Doctor Trevor Dixon, physiotherapist Terry Hayes and kit man Derek McKinley all played a vital part in the preparations and matches and were much valued members of the team.

4 WORLD CUP QUALIFYING GAMES
AZERBAIJAN AND AUSTRIA

Away games mean a lot of hard work and preparation for the international department of the IFA whose personnel organise player and staff travel arrangements, hotels, training facilities and menus.

David Currie, with the IFA for 13 years, is Head of International Administration. Lawrie was the fourth manager he had worked for after Bryan Hamilton, Lawrie McMenemy and Sammy McIlroy.

DAVID CURRIE:

"The managers have very different styles. They see and approach things differently. Lawrie emphasised discipline, preparation and attention to detail. He studied matches carefully. He knew what he was talking about.

"The players were left under no illusion about what he expected from them and their conduct on and off the pitch. Around the hotel for example, that sort of thing, and that got through to the players because the vast majority of them responded.

"He had a very professional approach and he expected the players to be the same. Maybe previously some players might have thought it was a wee break away from their clubs and stuff like that coming into international duty but Lawrie said they were here to win football matches not for a wee break.

"Lawrie prepared thoroughly for the matches. He studied the opposition, he was very into statistics. He watched the opposition, he viewed videos of their matches, he used the Scout Seven system to get details on players, he used ProZone analysis of games. He would know the strengths and weaknesses of the opposition because he had studied them.

"We had used Newforge in the past for coaching courses so we knew about the facilities there. It was just a matter of whether Lawrie wanted to travel that far from the team hotel, which is 30 to 40 minutes away. Once he started using it for training sessions we never moved away from there.

"I didn't usually discuss hotels and overseas training pitches with Lawrie. I knew what he wanted, I knew what the international team required. I don't think I ever booked a bad hotel for him. I would keep an eye out for particular things. Obviously if you're going to Eastern Europe you would make sure there were no ladies of the night hanging about hotels, which is quite a common occurrence in Eastern Europe. Those sorts of things.

"I remember in Azerbaijan the hotel was quite close to a traffic junction and the players' rooms were on the traffic junction and they couldn't get enough sleep.

"I would have to find a suitable room within the hotel for the press conferences and a private room for the players to eat in. I would try to ensure all the players' rooms were on one floor so that the kit could be distributed.

"The team doctor Trevor Dixon arranged all the food originally but then we used to adapt the menu occasionally. We sent all the menu requirements ahead to the hotel so they were prepared. Chicken and pasta, vegetables, carbohydrates particularly coming up to the game. There had to be a good choice because not everybody likes the same thing. And it's all buffet style, and there's plenty of it.

"Most of the players share a room, it's been a traditional thing but lately Lawrie had said that any players who had 50 caps could have a room of their own if they wished. Some of them did, more the senior players, which you can understand."

ABOVE: Lawrie with David Currie, IFA Head of International Administration, and former IFA president Jim Boyce.

David Currie worked closely with David Segel, managing director of West End Travel in London, England. David Segel has been the official travel agent of the IFA for 35 years and has worked with nine Northern Ireland managers if you count Billy Bingham twice.

DAVID SEGEL:

"Lawrie was looking for a standard of accommodation commensurate with a national team which we were always supplying anyway. He was particularly concerned with flight timings, that we weren't doing a crack of dawn or late at night job. He was also mindful of cost, he didn't come in willy nilly saying this is what I want regardless of cost and he would react favourably if we explained it could be cheaper doing it a particular way."

For home games the team continued to stay at the hotel about 30 minutes north of Belfast where they had stayed prior to Lawrie taking over. Home games were relatively straight forward for David Segel, as he simply had to organise players' flights into Northern Ireland. Away games required much more preparation.

IFA TRAVEL AGENT DAVID SEGEL:

"An away game involves research, we don't take anything by chance so it means David Currie and I go to the destination, wherever it is, several months ahead of a game and we look at the hotels, David looks at the training ground and the stadium, perhaps the British Embassy. Then we make our judgement. We are looking for a classy hotel which, if possible, is not too deep in the heart of the city centre, just outside. Often we will take recommendations from the local football association.

"We have to do a deal with the hotel, to get it for a price which is acceptable to the IFA and manageable within the budget and the earlier we go the more chance we have of getting precisely what we want.

"There are one or two players who have reservations about flying and certainly hold onto the sides of their seat when the plane takes off but generally no one has refused to fly because of fear.

"We have had one or two players in the past who have missed their flight, not due to being irresponsible but because the connection bringing them into Heathrow is delayed or due to traffic on the motorway getting to the airport.

"Luggage has been lost yes, invariably because we are moving with so much baggage. Today the nightmare isn't; are the hotels going to be okay? And will the flights go on time? Your nightmare is all about baggage, excess baggage, loss of baggage. These are the worries and concerns that we have.

"When we were flying to Azerbaijan from Heathrow we were taking a lot of people with us and all the media were there, and I had an extremely fat file. SKY wanted to interview Lawrie and he borrowed my file to hold while they interviewed him, and on the news that night I saw a report that said, 'As you can see, Lawrie Sanchez's preparation for this trip was amazing,' and they showed a close up picture of my file! My file, he gets the credit, good luck to him!"

PHOTOGRAPHER WILLIAM CHERRY:

"It doesn't take me long to prepare for a trip, my wife helps. We've got it down to a bit of a system actually – I pack up my gear and she does the rest. I try not to take too much, but I have to have my camera bag obviously, which holds two cameras, three lenses, three flashes and my laptop. There's a separate case for my 300mm lens for sport. In my case for clothes I'll also pack chargers for my phone and batteries, adapters, monopod, waterproofs, blank CDs, and a power bar. I'm not sure how much it weighs, but I'm always being charged for excess baggage.

"I've never lost anything – my equipment has been delayed a few times but it's always arrived in time to cover the matches. It is stressful travelling with so much equipment – it's always a relief to get to the hotel room with everything intact!"

9 OCTOBER 2004 – FIFA WORLD CUP 2006 QUALIFYING ROUNDS
AZERBAIJAN v NORTHERN IRELAND
BAKHRAMOV NATIONAL STADIUM, BAKU
RESULT: DRAW 0–0
ATTENDANCE: 6,460

LAWRIE SANCHEZ:

"Keith [Gillespie] changed from being very anti what we were attempting to do to being very pro it. In fact he converted to what we wanted to do more so than anybody else at the end of the day. He changed with Azerbaijan away.

"Keith was left out of the initial squad for that game and when the squad was announced everyone was asking, 'Is this the end of Keith Gillespie's international career?' and I said, no it wasn't.

"Because of squad drop-outs Keith was called in at the last minute and I said to David [Currie], 'I don't think he'll turn up.' But to be fair to him he did without any question. I think we only took 17 players.

"He was on the bench. After four or five minutes the right back Chris Baird got injured and Keith went to right back and from that moment on he played in every game under me.

"That was a turning point for me. I hadn't tried to get him out of the squad but he was fighting me with his body language about what we were attempting to do; which was silly really because it suited him more than anybody because I like wingers and he was a good winger, and we were trying to get the ball to him to get lots of crosses and he crosses a good ball. But he played really well in that game and from then on he was a permanent fixture in the side and went on to be one of the best players.

"We didn't have David Healy in the Azerbaijan game because of his red card in Wales and that meant we didn't really have a goal scorer. We drew 0–0 so it was a good result but if we'd had David Healy we would have won that game with the chances we created. The loss of David Healy not only lost us two points in Wales but also two points from Azerbaijan.

"Azerbaijan was the first introduction to Steve Davis. He came along with us because of the pull outs. He impressed us in training that week. We took him and Brunty [Chris] along, two young kids. We were impressed in training by what we saw from the pair of them, but certainly Steve stood out, we thought, 'God, this could be one for the future.' What we didn't realise was just how quickly he would be one, not in the future, it was immediate."

Keith Gillespie is a firm favourite with Northern Ireland fans. The passion he feels when playing for his country is obvious as soon as he pulls the green and white shirt on. One of his all-time heroes, admired from watching old videos, is George Best and Keith's teammates call him Bestie.

KEITH GILLESPIE:

"It was my dream as a kid to play for Northern Ireland, it means everything to me. I have 75 caps now and I just want to keep going for as long as I can. You get players who retire from international football but I don't think I would ever retire; it would just be a case of not being picked again.

"Lawrie and I had a few run-in's but I am full of praise for the job that he did. When he first came into the squad and took over as manager a lot of the players weren't too sure about the style of football but we were all proved wrong by the results we achieved. I have nothing but admiration for the fact he took us from 124 in the world to 29, which we are today [July 2007].

"I wasn't in the squad for Azerbaijan originally but a lot of players pulled out and I got pulled in and I played and went on to play every game since then."

Kate Hoey MP enjoys meeting Northern Ireland supporters as they travel around the world to matches and often sits with them.

KATE HOEY MP:

"Azerbaijan was the furthest one that we'd gone to and as we later went on to become more successful the number of away supporters increased. But in Azerbaijan you could have literally met every single supporter. There was a lot of mingling afterwards in the hotel between the players and the manager and the fans and that's something that I've always liked about Northern Ireland. There hasn't been that prima donna attitude.

"I remember there was a security guy there from England because they were playing Azerbaijan a few days afterwards and he was out there to check things. And I said to him, 'You won't be having all this easy going atmosphere in the bar after the match.' [Journalist, Dr] Malcolm Brodie was standing talking to Lawrie who was standing talking to some of the supporters who were in wearing all their gear. The players had gone up to their rooms, changed and come down and were mingling and were very accessible. Our fans are very good at knowing the barriers between giving them space and being friendly. And this security guy said, 'Goodness, we don't let anybody into the hotel.'

"I like the fact that we are a small country and can do it our way, although I appreciate that slightly changed towards the end as we became more successful, but there was still a rapport between the players and the fans."

13 OCTOBER 2004 – FIFA WORLD CUP 2006 QUALIFYING ROUNDS
NORTHERN IRELAND v AUSTRIA
WINDSOR PARK, BELFAST
RESULT: DRAW 3–3
(DAVID HEALY, COLIN MURDOCK, STUART ELLIOTT)
ATTENDANCE: 11,810

NI GOALKEEPING COACH DAVE BEASANT:

"I can remember us going behind in the first half and the equaliser was a David Healy special. I think it was the best goal he's ever scored for Northern Ireland. I remember the ball coming to him outside the box, and he was facing away from the goal and his first touch wasn't a great touch and he turned and on his unfavoured left foot he just hit this volley, and it looked as if it was going ten yards over the crossbar but it went up and down so quickly it dipped. Alex Manniger, the Arsenal goalkeeper for Austria, could just stand and look at it. It was an unbelievable goal. The best Northern Ireland individual goal.

"We came in at half time 1–1 and things were looking good. This was a qualifier at home to Austria, we had gone a goal down, and previously when we'd been a goal down we wouldn't play well, we had never managed to drag a victory from the jaws of defeat. So to crawl back to a draw at half time was a positive.

"During half time Lawrie tended to give the boys a couple of minutes to themselves while he walked off to assess his thoughts. We had a dressing room, it was more like a skip room under the stand, it wasn't the nicest accommodation for the manager and the coaching staff, cold wooden floor, right under the stand, so the room sloped and got smaller and smaller. You can imagine which end I changed at and which end Gibbo changed at!

"So Lawrie would go into this room and have a bit of time to himself and the boys would be a bit vocal to each other. Maybe me and Gibbo would go around and say a few individual things, and then Lawrie would come in and speak to them as a team about

things they didn't do so well and what he wanted them to try and do more of. He would get his points over, ask if there were any questions or whether there were any problems, we would try and put them right and then leave the last couple of minutes to the boys. The boys did their psychological thing in geeing each other up and motivating each other.

"Colin got the second goal from a corner. I think Keith took the corner and Colin rose like a salmon and he headed one. And actually if you look at it, I know Dave has never tried to claim it, but Dave was standing in front of the goalkeeper and as Colin headed it, it flipped off Dave Healy's arm and went in. Dave didn't put his arm out, it just clipped his arm so technically it came off him and if he wanted to claim another goal he probably could.

"But Murdo doesn't score too many goals and he's mild mannered and quite collected in what he does and for Colin he let himself go a little bit. That was down at the Kop Stand.

"For us to take the lead was significant. But as we'd done in our first game against Norway, when we were 3–0 down and scored our first goal in two years we were so busy celebrating they got another one, and the same thing happened here.

"Austria equalised, it had a negative impact on the team, then Austria went on to score a third goal. We were throwing everything forward, the referee put up three minutes of injury time. We had everyone in the box and Stuart Elliott got an equaliser in the last minute. The Austrian keeper got a dislocated shoulder from his dive. A draw was a great result."

At the end of 2003 David Bowen left the IFA.

FORMER IFA GENERAL SECRETARY DAVID BOWEN:

"My own memories of being Lawrie's employer are from his first year in office. I could see the whole change in the squad and the beginning of a better squad who might qualify. I saw Lawrie as a breath of fresh air.

"We have spoken since he got the Fulham job and he thanked me for getting him back on the managerial ladder, and I thanked him for being so kind as to ring me and remember that. We have a very

ABOVE: Stuart Elliott's equaliser against Austria at Windsor Park taking the final score line to a 3–3 draw with the other goals from David Healy and Colin Murdock.

good relationship and a personal friendship and indeed when I left my own job at the IFA Lawrie Sanchez was one of the very few people that sent me a nice gift to thank me for my little help to him. I was delighted to hear from him when he got his full-time job at Fulham because I always knew that was where he would be most happy, in full-time club employment.

"I can only look back on very happy days with him and continued friendship."

LAWRIE SANCHEZ:

"I got on well with David. He said to me when I took over, 'Look Lawrie all you need to do is run the first team, that's your job. Keep out of the politics of Northern Ireland, win some football matches, it's nice and simple.'

"I was sorry to see him go. He was on my side. I have great respect for David."

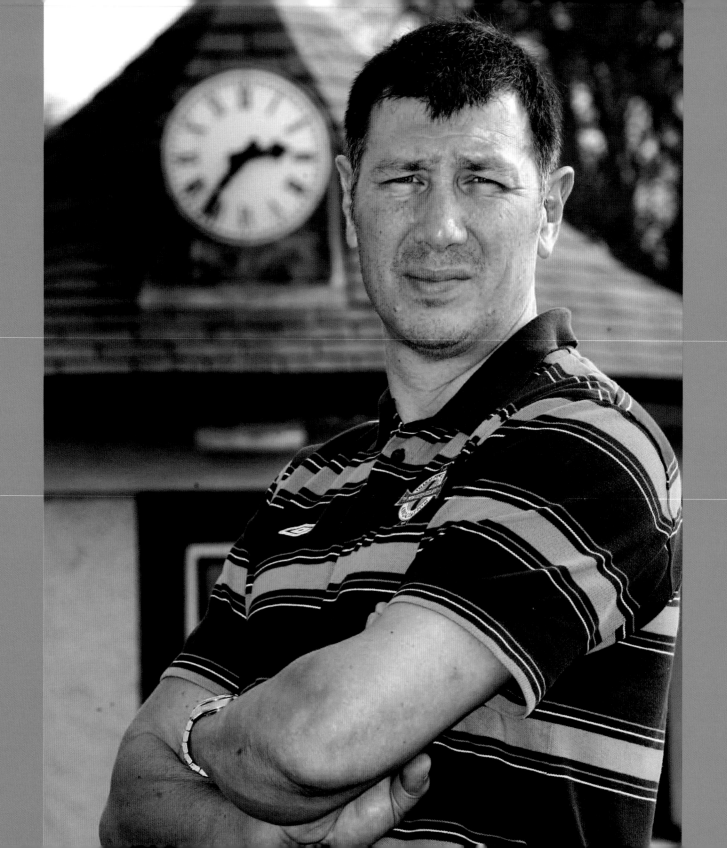

5 A NEW CHIEF EXECUTIVE

In January 2005 Englishman Howard Wells was installed as the first chief executive of the Irish Football Association.

Howard brought a wealth of sports experience to the province. He was a former chief executive of the Hong Kong Sports Institute, the Hong Kong Sports Development Board, the UK Sports Council and Watford and Ipswich football clubs.

LAWRIE SANCHEZ:

"I didn't know Howard. I met him soon after his appointment in the January.

"He was at a function at Bisham Abbey and I said I'd come over and meet him at The Compleat Angler Hotel in Marlow [Buckinghamshire, England]. We had an initial discussion about what he intended to do.

"I literally said to Howard, 'Look you've got an awful lot of corners to fight. I know how to run the first team.'

"We'd progressed a certain number of positions in the world, I think we'd gone up about 19 or 20 places in my first year in charge. I said, 'I know how to run the international side after a year's experience. Leave it to myself working with David Currie, we'll take care of that. And you can worry about all the other issues you'll have to deal with.'"

I knew Howard from his days at Watford FC and when he was appointed to the IFA he called to ask if I would be interested in running the communications department. I was not able to take on the job permanently but offered to do three days a week for six months until

Belfast-based personnel could be installed. I also knew Lawrie, from his time managing Wycombe and we spoke on the telephone before I started working in Belfast.

It was an important year for the IFA, celebrating the 125th anniversary, hosting the UEFA Under-19 Tournament and taking part in the FIFA World Cup 2006 qualifying games. Howard instructed me to "love the press to pieces". The IFA did not have a great track record with the media and Howard wanted to reverse the trend, to be as transparent as possible and embrace them. My work would involve media relations, the website, programme and press office. It was apparent there were people currently in all these roles. My job was temporary and I did not want any of them to feel they were being usurped. Howard assured me that the press officer Denise Ward welcomed my imminent arrival and I was pleased to find this was the case when we spoke on the telephone several times over the weeks prior to my flying over to Belfast.

The office Denise and I shared was right at the back of the building in Windsor Avenue with very little in it. On the day I arrived, my desk beneath the window had a wobbly leg, no telephone and the drawers were broken. I had no pens, paper, stapler or waste paper basket. There was a very ancient computer, no calendar of events to show what all the team fixtures were, no office diary for appointments, no press cuttings, no newspapers. Denise didn't have a business card.

The only way was up.

9 FEBRUARY 2005 – INTERNATIONAL FRIENDLY MATCH
NORTHERN IRELAND v CANADA
WINDSOR PARK, BELFAST
RESULT: LOST 1–0
ATTENDANCE: 11,156

IFA CHIEF EXECUTIVE HOWARD WELLS:

"It appeared to be a very disjointed performance where Northern Ireland were 'undone' by a header from a free kick. I thought, 'this is going to be a long three years', which was the length of my contract."

The match against Canada was the first time I saw the squad in action, and the first time I witnessed the passion unleashed in Windsor Park, that great 100-year-old stadium in south Belfast, home to Linfield Football Club and rented out to the IFA for international matches. I discovered it was quite easy to walk to the stadium from the IFA offices and did so often during my time there, sauntering down the streets of old-fashioned terraced housing and across the huge iron railway bridge where murals of favoured sons cover the dusty brick walls.

The stadium absorbed almost 60,000 fans in the days of terracing but now seats just over 14,000. It reminded me of non-league grounds in England, old fashioned with a great atmosphere and stands placed very close to the pitch.

The press box was way up in the South Stand, covered thankfully, and with desks for the front and middle rows. It seats 49 but only 32 have telephone lines and power points and the back row has a restricted view. Seventy seats were allocated outside as a press overflow area for big matches, 16 of which could be served by telephone. With such big matches coming up later in the year the facilities were going to be seriously stretched.

The Linfield FC Members Lounge was used as a press room on match days, where photographers and reporters could file pictures and stories with the aid of BT Openzone which Denise had had installed; and where Lawrie gave his post-match interviews. But the biggest problem was the lack of a mixed-zone area.

This was an area that Denise and the Northern Ireland Football Writers Association had brought to my attention as a matter requiring urgent attention. UEFA rules stated such a zone has to be in place for all international matches, to enable players to walk through a cordoned off area where the media can ask them questions. The players do not have to stop, but they are required to walk through it. With Germany and England coming to town their media posses would not be best pleased to find such a facility lacking.

It was an issue which took up much of my time, meetings and energy.

NI GOALKEEPING COACH DAVE BEASANT:

"We felt that we needed a game because of the gap between qualifiers. We looked at the fixture and felt it would be a morale booster with a victory at home at Windsor Park in front of the fans. It turned out to be a shocking night with swirly winds and horrible conditions. They got a free kick, one of their boys got on the end of it, whipped it in, goal. Because they'd got their lead, they just sat back and soaked up the pressure and when you've got ten men behind the ball it's really hard to break a team down.

"So what we were looking for, a morale booster, positive victory, score some goals, a win at home which we hadn't had yet, it didn't happen and went the exact opposite way.

"Everyone was deflated. I think that was one of the first games you could see the fans were disappointed with what they'd seen.

"It was a bit of a disappointing fixture in the end.

"Myself and Lawrie started our playing careers in the lower divisions so we know what it's like to play around second and third division grounds. Then when you have the luxury of playing in the Premier Division and the Championship you have great facilities, lovely stadiums. Although the Kop Stand and the North Stands are nice stands, Windsor Park still reminded me a bit of a good, non-league ground. It wasn't a fantastic ground, the dressing rooms are tiny and not very welcoming. But the fact was, once those Northern Ireland fans got inside the ground they made it a very, very welcoming place for us, and a very intimidating place for the opposition.

"There was a similar scenario when we played for Wimbledon at Plough Lane, it was even smaller, half the size of Windsor Park and we didn't have a stand like the Kop Stand. But we knew that when teams like Man United came down to Plough Lane they looked at the place and thought, 'What the hell are we doing here?'

"I know in the international set up there are countries with small international stadiums like the Faroe Isles and Liechtenstein but the facilities are quite good over there. Windsor was an unwelcoming place for opposing teams to come to and sometimes I think even our players were looking at it and thinking, 'Oh flipping hell,' and would have preferred a nice stadium to play in.

"But the fact was 14,000 fans making the noise they did made it sound like there were 30,000 fans there. Sometimes it's better to have a full house and the atmosphere that's generated in a small stadium than having a 60,000 all-seater and only 25,000 people there because it doesn't create the atmosphere.

"We found that we tended to play better, and the atmosphere was better, with evening kick-off's. Because it's dark you don't see the gaps in the corners of the stands. More often than not we were playing over the winter period and on a cold, wet night the fans were up for it and we were up for it. We wanted a high tempo game and demanded a work rate and effort from the players that was a lot harder to do on a really sunny day. The heat can drain you and make you lethargic and tired.

"I know Lawrie had changed all our kick-off times to evenings for the rest of the Euro 2008 campaign. He wanted them playing at night rather than three o'clock in the afternoon. So it was cooler, darker, we tended to respond better.

"In football nowadays because players get a bit hyper and don't sleep very well a lot of times they take a form of sleeping tablet. If they don't get a good night's rest they're not going to perform next day. Sometimes they have a good night's sleep and at three o'clock it might not be totally out of their system, so with a few more hours they would be a lot more alive."

6 WORLD CUP QUALIFYING GAMES
ENGLAND AND POLAND

When the pot was drawn for the World Cup qualifiers, the game everyone was waiting for was this. Playing England at Manchester United's Old Trafford ground would be quite some experience. Playing at Wembley might have been even better, but with the new London stadium still under construction the national team were travelling around the country to play at various Premiership grounds.

The week before we all met up in Manchester, Lawrie and I went to the headquarters of The Football Association in Soho Square, London. He was to have a head-to-head with England coach Sven Goran Eriksson before the media. We had a few familiar friendly faces there from the Northern Ireland press, but it was primarily the English dailies and broadcasters.

Lawrie and Sven sat on a podium at the top of the room, Lawrie looking confident, imposing and stylish in a new striped suit.

LAWRIE SANCHEZ:

"The day before we met up I was informed that Sven was ill and he might not be able to take part, and I thought the media were not coming to talk to me they were coming to talk to Sven, and if he wasn't there it would be a bit of a damp squib. But he turned up, we had a good chat before the meeting and we did the press conference. In the middle of it he had to leave, and one of the

reporters asked if he was upset because of the question that had just been asked, and he was told, 'No Sven has gone out to throw up because he's not very well.'

"Sven was very gracious, very good to me and I have great respect for him."

Lawrie knew of a country house hotel, Mottram Hall, on the outskirts of Manchester where he had stayed during his playing days with Wimbledon. In the grounds was a specialist football pitch laid in 1996 to the exact dimensions of Wembley for the German team who stayed there during the European Cup qualifiers that year. Germany then went on to win that tournament. Lawrie visited with David Currie to check it over, and the place was booked as our base during the trip to the north-west of England.

I had arranged to have a team picture taken here on the manicured rolling lawns. This was because soon after I arrived at the IFA I had asked Michael Boyd (then the IFA community relations officer, now head of that department) to survey the fans about their feelings on the match day programmes. Their comments were positive but one thing they specifically requested was a team poster as a pull-out.

This was my first trip away with the squad, and it was a great way to get to know the players properly. I took the opportunity to create profiles on almost every one of them during the time we were together, to ensure I had all their facts and figures at my fingertips in readiness for media enquires.

The press were all staying at the hotel with us which did surprise me.

OPPOSITE: Later to be voted the best fans in Europe, the GAWA never stopped singing throughout the 4–0 defeat to England at Old Trafford.

The official press conferences and open training sessions, where photographers were allowed to take pictures of the players during the first 15 minutes of training, seemed rather pointless as the media had open access to the players all day and into the evening as we were all sharing the same bars, lounges and bumping into one another in corridors.

However, the atmosphere was congenial and everyone seemed to get on well. Some of the media and players had been travelling together for years and had an easy understanding of one another. On the whole the media didn't bother the team for interviews outside the official meetings.

Over in the England camp things were done very differently. Denise and I went to visit one of their press conferences and found that where we used one room for press events the FA used several. The largest was set up with lighting and a catwalk to enable some of the senior players to model the new team strip and meet competition winners. Another room was set up specifically for television interviews and we

watched David Beckham answering questions whilst sitting next to an FA press officer.

Lots of smaller rooms off a long corridor were set up for individual television broadcasters to conduct one to one interviews; and there was a reception area where journalists were eating, drinking and working on their laptops. Around there I distributed leaflets I had been working on which explained the nature of football in Northern Ireland and a little about the association, Howard and Lawrie.

During our stay in Manchester, Lawrie renewed his contract and agreed to remain with the IFA until November 2007.

Before every international match the opposing team has a training session in the match day stadium to work on the pitch and get a feel for it. So on Friday we all travelled to Old Trafford in the team bus, and while the boys trained on the pitch Denise and I were shown around the press facilities, seeing the press box and the locations for the post-match

ABOVE: The squad photograph taken at Mottram Hall near Manchester with backroom and support staff.

TV and print interviews. I was interested to see that even in a stadium as modern as Old Trafford there was no specifically constructed area for the mixed zone; it was created manually with the aid of road barriers at the end of the tunnel, leading to the players' coach.

The occasion must have been particularly poignant for David Healy, Keith Gillespie and Colin Murdock who had all played with Manchester United during their careers.

DAVID HEALY:

"I was actually lucky enough to play at Old Trafford so to go back there and see some of the people I had known, the groundsmen and catering staff, it was very, very nice and I felt very proud walking out onto the pitch the next day to play there again."

26 MARCH 2005 – FIFA WORLD CUP 2006 QUALIFYING ROUNDS
ENGLAND v NORTHERN IRELAND
OLD TRAFFORD STADIUM, MANCHESTER
RESULT: LOST 4–0
ATTENDANCE: 62,239

LAWRIE SANCHEZ:

"We'd had a great week's training and were excellent in the first half, coming in at half time 0–0. We had done everything we had set out to do. We'd been resilient, defending our own goal, done everything right. Although we hadn't caused too many problems at the other end we'd restricted England which is what we intended to do.

"We then went out in the second half and shot ourselves in the foot from the word go. Giving goals away with basic errors, rather than making them have to score. We gave three goals away in eleven minutes. Then it was a matter of damage limitation.

ABOVE: IFA chief executive Howard Wells and former IFA president Jim Boyce with Lawrie as he signs an extension to his contract at the team hotel, Mottram Hall, prior to playing England at Old Trafford

BELOW: Lawrie and Gerry at the press conference prior to playing England.

ABOVE: Sven Goran Eriksson and Lawrie chat during their teams' training sessions at Old Trafford the day before meeting in the World Cup qualifiers.
RIGHT: Dave and Lawrie training near Manchester.

"Old Trafford is an excellent stadium and our fans made some fantastic noise. I think we took 6,500 people and David Beckham said after the game he'd not heard singing like that before, which is a great credit to the fans especially when we were 4–0 down and they were singing, 'We're going to win 5–4.'

"This match was Steve Davis' debut for Northern Ireland. He replaced Tommy Doherty and in the half hour he was on the pitch he showed he was not just one for the future, he was one for now. From then on he was a regular, ever present, going on to be the youngest ever captain of Northern Ireland when we went on the summer tour of America in 2006."

PICTURES THIS PAGE: Training at Mottram Hall near Manchester.

KEITH GILLESPIE:

"It was nice to be back at Old Trafford, it's a fantastic stadium to play in. It was just a shame that we didn't do ourselves justice, particularly in the second half. I think the Northern Ireland fans that day were just absolutely incredible, they sang from start to finish and got behind us."

On this double header away trip I had the opportunity to get to know not only the players but the media including the legendary Dr Malcolm Brodie, Gordon Hanna, Steven Beacom (*Belfast Telegraph*), Orla Bannon (*Daily Mirror*), Paul Ferguson (*Sunday Life*) and UTV sports reporter Claire McCollum and her cameraman Albert Kirk. In addition, our party included several correspondents from the English nationals who became familiar, friendly faces, including John Edwards (*Daily Mail*) and

LEFT: Northern Ireland backroom staff Dr Trevor Dixon and physiotherapist Terry Hayes, during training at Old Trafford the day before facing England.
BELOW: Lawrie at Old Trafford.

William Johnston (*Daily Telegraph*) as well as Ken Gaunt from the Press Association. To a man the English reporters always stressed how much they enjoyed travelling with Northern Ireland.

On arrival in Poland we all stayed in an impressive modern hotel in the centre of Warsaw, within walking distance of the Ghetto Hero's Memorial to the Jewish people who suffered so badly in the Second World War; and the historic Old Town which was almost completely destroyed during the same period, but was subsequently rebuilt to look like the original and is now inscribed on UNESCO's (United Nations Educational, Scientific and Cultural Organisation) World Heritage List.

KATE HOEY MP:

"One of the nice things that Lawrie always did was to make sure, when we were on away matches, that the players had the opportunity to get out for a little bit to see some of the history. For example in Warsaw they all went to see the museums to the Jewish people who had been killed. I thought it was very good that the manager set an example by getting the players to go and see something so that they know they are in Poland and not, for example, Glasgow.

"Lawrie is a very intelligent person and slightly different to the normal stereotype of a football manager; very knowledgeable and cultured and well educated, which meant he had a wider interest in things than what one might assume the normal manager has.

"I love football but I'm not a football coach so in terms of how he managed and coached the team I have no knowledge of that except that whatever he did he got them to believe in themselves and that they could actually win. He has the capacity to motivate and he clearly likes and enjoys working with almost being the underdog, to play well beyond what is seen as their normal possibilities."

30 MARCH 2005 – FIFA WORLD CUP 2006 QUALIFYING ROUNDS
POLAND v NORTHERN IRELAND
LEGIA STADIUM, WARSAW
RESULT: LOST 1–0
ATTENDANCE: 13,515

ABOVE: Steve Jones and Andy Kirk enjoying the sights of Warsaw.

ABOVE: Lawrie with Terry Gibson and Dave Beasant at training in Poland.

LAWRIE SANCHEZ:

"This was my most disappointing game. People talk about losing 3–0 to Poland in the opening game in Belfast, and to Iceland in the opening game of the Euro's, but we played so well in this game.

"Coming on the back of a 4–0 defeat against England it was a matter of picking the lads up. The biggest thing they showed was resilience, we picked ourselves up, we did a professional job in Poland. We held the Polish team for 87 minutes, and in fact the players were so confident that we were going to get a win that we got caught on the break. The ball went down the other end, they took a quick corner and scored from it and to be honest that was the most gutted I ever was as Northern Ireland manager.

"We played so, so well and it was a hammer blow to get beaten in that last three or four minutes. We went away numb from there. For me in my 32 games with Northern Ireland that was the lowest for me."

ABOVE: An heroic save from Northern Ireland goalkeeper Maik Taylor in Poland.

BELOW: Disappointment following the last minute defeat.

NI SUPPORTER ALAN FERRIS:

"We members of the GAWA thoroughly enjoyed our time in Poland's capital, but not the result. The last minute goal gave Poland victory. The manager looked deflated, as did the players but the GAWA were not quietened. We continued to sing Lawrie's praises for 20 minutes after the game finished. Some of us were staying in the same hotel as the team in Warsaw and we were delighted that Lawrie and his team mingled with the fans. While firm and ardent in his view and approach in all aspects of football, Lawrie recognised that the fans were a very important factor in his plans. He chatted with us, posed for photographs and signed autographs. He was fast becoming a fans' favourite."

125TH ANNIVERSARY

GERMANY AND MALTA

A lot of people worked extremely hard to make the anniversary year a success. Preparing Windsor Park for any international match is a huge job, preparing it for the arrival of a big country like Germany is even bigger.

William Campbell has worked for the IFA for 24 years. When I first met him his job title was Head of Finance and Personnel, but he was also responsible for match arrangements, ticketing, refereeing and security. Most people at the IFA stoically juggled several jobs. Following Howard Wells' restructuring William's job title later changed to Head of Operations.

WILLIAM CAMPBELL:

"The England match was the one everyone was very excited about when the World Cup draw was made because England hadn't played in Belfast since 1987, 18 years previously. England bring their own set of problems, with fans, security and the high profile nature of the players, Rooney and Beckham and so on. The German match, which had been arranged as a celebration of the IFA's 125th anniversary, gave us an ideal opportunity to put in place in June the plans for a full stadium with 1,000 visiting fans, which was the maximum number allowed, and then replicate it again in September when England came.

"The planning for the Germany match started in early spring. We have a basic plan for spectators, how to get them in and out,

OPPOSITE: Damien Johnson battles for the ball against Germany's Thomas Hitzisperger during the International Challenge Match at Windsor Park to mark the 125th anniversary of the Irish Football Association.

security and so on, which we adjust depending on if you're playing Azerbaijan who bring nobody, or whether you're playing England or Germany who bring the maximum number.

"We put into place all the ticket checking and the security inside and outside the stadium. We had several meetings with the local police, with the safety officer from Belfast City Council who issued a safety certificate and with the security company.

"On the morning of the game we always have a meeting at the stadium to run through the arrangements for the match. The delegate for the game checks that everything has been done; that the visiting team have had an opportunity to train on the pitch; that the referees have had an opportunity to see the ground and make sure everything is in place.

"Visiting teams always have a training session on the stadium pitch the day before the game to give them a feel for the ground and usually at the same time as kick-off will be, so that if it is an evening game and they will be playing under lights the players have an opportunity to see how good the floodlights are, to get their eyes used to the glare, because every set of lights is slightly different.

"Likewise every football is different. We play with Umbro footballs and therefore give Umbro balls to all opposition teams to use in their training sessions in Belfast. They might come from a country that uses Mitre or Addidas.

"Every visiting team has a liaison officer, which is organised between myself and David Currie. We have a pool of people we use, and it is the job of the liaison officer to be with the visiting team at all times and that person would contact David or me with any problems, depending on what the problems were.

"The Germans had problems with their supporters. They were

keen that the proper security was in place. They had brought some German police with them who were undercover mingling with the German supporters to make sure there were no hooligans and that they all behaved themselves, and also to be in a better position to identify any known troublemakers to our police, to keep an eye on them.

"They came over two or three days before the game and they were staying with, and being looked after by, the PSNI [Police Service of Northern Ireland]. Our police are doing similar now when we travel abroad.

"The Germans had an added problem in that their [football association] president was very unpopular and they were very keen to ensure that any banners put up by German fans were not offensive, and that their president would be properly safe and secure getting into and out of the stadium; where would he be sitting, who would be sitting beside him, that sort of thing.

"Windsor Park is an old stadium, over 100 years old. It was not built as one entity. New stadia now are built with a definite plan; Windsor Park was built like Lego where they built one stand, and then they built another stand many years later so it's not very well coordinated, there's not great access throughout the stadium. It's old and it's tired and that gives us problems.

"At a high-profile, top match we would have inside the stadium somewhere in the region of 30 to 40 police. Outside the stadium, on traffic and general duties with the crowd plus a contingency of police on standby in case of problems, there would probably be another 100 policemen.

"We would have approximately 250 stewards. I was responsible for them all.

"Sometimes in the run up to a game your mind would be playing tricks with you, but normally the night before everything is in place, there's nothing more you can do it's just a matter of turning up on the day and getting everything done. All the planning is done, I have a very good team of people that I work with and trust. That gives you security and the fact that we've been doing it for so long together. You can almost pre-empt what each other is thinking about.

"I do my best to be in a position to see a lot of the football.

Sometimes something turns up and I have to go and deal with it. I'm either in the police post or down on pitch side during most of the second half. I would commence the game in the director's area ensuring that all the directors are in place. I do my best to see most of the game, 60 or 70 per cent on a good night, perhaps 50 per cent on not such a good night."

My priorities were to get the new IFA website launched for the Germany game; to ensure the mixed zone worked; to get the team poster into the match day programme; and to see the beginnings of our Junior Supporters scheme.

With the help of Martin Harris and Marshall Gillespie I had been working for months on phase one of the new website, which was filled with fabulous images and lots of editorial content. Essential add-on's such as on-line ticketing and dedicated supporters' areas, which we were all keen to see, were expected to be developed later when a commercial appointment was made.

The mixed zone issue had been resolved and was to be in the Members' Lounge of Windsor Park. Prior to kick-off the same room was used for the inaugural hot media meal, or as William Campbell liked to label it: "Heather Jan's party". The media worked very hard at matches and were under tight deadlines, often staying at the stadium hours after the final whistle. The hot meal became a regular part of all international home matches; and was supplemented with light refreshments at half time.

There were a number of us who never saw the beginning of the second half of matches played at Windsor because as soon as the media had all gone back to the press box it was all hands on deck to clear the room of tables, chairs and catering equipment and to replace it with barriers, sponsor's branding and cordoned off areas to turn it into a pretty reasonable mixed zone.

The team poster taken in Manchester was in situ in the souvenir, match-day programme edited by *News Letter* journalist and author Billy Kennedy; and the Junior Supporters Scheme was launched.

IFA president Jim Boyce was very keen to see some lasting legacies of the anniversary year and I am a great believer in encouraging children to come to football matches. I had started up a Junior Supporters scheme at the first club I worked at and decided to replicate it as my contribution towards the celebration of 125 years of the IFA.

The scheme took off at the Germany game with one of the benefits of membership being the chance to be a match mascot. It was Dawn Smyth's job to look after the mascots.

4 JUNE 2005 – INTERNATIONAL FRIENDLY MATCH TO CELEBRATE THE 125TH ANNIVERSARY OF THE IRISH FOOTBALL ASSOCIATION
NORTHERN IRELAND v GERMANY
WINDSOR PARK, BELFAST
RESULT: LOST 4–1
(DAVID HEALY)
ATTENDANCE: 14,000

ABOVE: Stuart Elliott, in the background, salutes David Healy's goal against Germany.

ABOVE: Lawrie, his staff and some of the players in the dug out prior to kick-off against Germany in the 125th anniversary friendly match at Windsor Park, Belfast.

LAWRIE SANCHEZ:

"I remember when I got the job Bobby Gould, my former manager at Wimbledon, said to me, 'Whatever you do don't ever allow them to organise prestige friendlies because you'll probably get beaten badly and when they add up your results at the end of your time nobody will take into account that you played Germany, Portugal, any of these teams. They'll just say, well you lost those games.'

"We had a makeshift team. We went in front for about 40 seconds, David Healy scored a penalty and we were in front and I was thinking, 'Cor, we could beat Germany.' And then they went off down the other end and scored and it was 1–1 and then in the second half, even with one man less, they dominated and beat us.

"It was a good night, it was a celebration, the crowd enjoyed it. But I always remember Bobby Gould's words."

ABOVE: Stephen Craigan wins the ball.

Defender Stephen Craigan earned his first caps under Sammy McIlroy but it was under Lawrie that his international career really took off. For the friendly against Germany he was in the starting line-up.

STEPHEN CRAIGAN:

"I have 29 caps most of them under Lawrie. I've started every international game since Germany.

"When Lawrie took the job he held a meeting with the players and said if we were loyal to the country and the jersey and did well we would stay in the team. He was very loyal to me and I found him to be a man of his word. I trusted him and felt he believed in his players."

This was to be Denise's last game. We had held an official farewell at Windsor Avenue and had another for the media during the meal before kick-off.

FORMER IFA PRESS OFFICER DENISE WARD:

"I don't know how relevant this is but I was brought up as a Catholic in Derry City and most people would have expected me to support the Republic football team rather than Northern Ireland. For me to pledge my allegiance to Northern Ireland and say I am a fan is quite something. I never get up to Windsor to see the boys these days, but I'm never far from the TV when a game is being shown live.

"I left the IFA in June because of hangovers from the previous regime. I had felt undervalued. I spoke to Howard about it and I know he was changing things but it wasn't changing fast enough for me. I can see now the fantastic changes he has made but at the time I had just had enough.

"Germany was my last game and I wanted to say goodbye to Lawrie but everything is always so rushed and busy after a game and there wasn't time. Two days later I received a voice message on my phone from Lawrie wishing me all the best in my new job. I thought that was nice, I wish I had saved it for longer in my saved messages."

As one face leaves another arrives, and just prior to the Germany game Paul Prentice joined the backroom staff to help physio Terry Hayes out in the treatment room.

Paul was a schoolboy goalkeeper and played alongside some of the international stars when he was a boy in the Lisburn Youth team. He later studied for a diploma in Sports Massage Therapy and works as a firemen during the day managing to get away for international football duty by taking annual leave.

PAUL PRENTICE:

"The majority of my work mates think I've got a great job with the team and they're very envious of me I think, especially now Northern Ireland are doing so well and I can be part of the atmosphere and the squad. I think any Northern Ireland fan would be envious of the position. I would be myself if I wasn't in it!

"As I used to be a schoolboy goalkeeper I guess Maik Taylor was my hero out of the current squad, but my all time hero was Pat Jennings. It was a great honour to meet all the players because they all contribute equally. A lot of the players I played with in youth teams growing up; David Healy, Damien Johnson, Warren Feeney, Aaron Hughes. Being part of the Northern Ireland squad and seeing all the guys again was good for me, to see how they were doing and to be part of their environment.

"There are no egos there, all the players, and especially the players who maybe have good reason to have an ego because of the publicity and how well we've done, are still very humble about the fact that they and the team are doing so well. They don't brag about it or show off or make anybody else feel uncomfortable. And I think that helps to instil a good team spirit and camaraderie."

Later in the summer during July Northern Ireland hosted the UEFA Under-19 Tournament. The Europa Hotel in central Belfast was the nerve centre of all preparations where UEFA and IFA officials were based together under the leadership of IFA tournament director Craig Stanfield with the eight teams who took part in the competition: Northern Ireland, England, France, Germany, Norway, Serbia and Montenegro, Armenia and Norway.

ABOVE: Lawrie with former IFA president Jim Boyce and international football legend Michel Platini making the draw for the UEFA Under-19 tournament at Belfast City Hall.

The matches were played at five grounds: Windsor Park; The Oval in Belfast; Ballymena Showgrounds; Newry Showgrounds; and Mournview Park in Lurgan.

During this fortnight came the historic announcement from the IRA that they intended to put down their arms. I visited the Falls and Shankhill roads covered with flags, murals and coloured kerb stones. These were places I had heard so much about, and watched on television during the desperate days of the Troubles and now here I was, standing in calm streets decorated with fluttering bunting. Several television crews were setting up outside broadcast units.

LAWRIE SANCHEZ:

"I did some match appraisals for the IFA technical department during the Under-19 Tournament.

"The final was between France and England and the French player Lassana Diarra is now at Arsenal. He was truly outstanding, a man amongst boys. France fully deserved to win the game and he was the outstanding player of the tournament.

"It was a good thing for Northern Ireland to organise a tournament like that. There were good crowds for it and it showed that although we're a small country we can do things right."

Later in the summer, on Thursday 7 July, I was at work in Belfast when the London bombs went off. Howard Wells and I were the only English people working at Windsor Avenue. There was a television in the Trophy Room and some of my colleagues had switched it on for news coverage of the events taking place in the capital city of England. Watching it with them brought home to me the terrors they had lived through for so much of their lives.

17 AUGUST 2005 – INTERNATIONAL FRIENDLY MATCH
MALTA v NORTHERN IRELAND
TA'QALI NATIONAL STADIUM, VALLETTA
RESULT: DRAW 1–1
(DAVID HEALY)
ATTENDANCE: 1,850

LAWRIE SANCHEZ:

"I said to the players, 'This is one that could produce a real sting in the tail for you. The days of beating Malta 6–0 are gone.' And so it turned out. They scored first and we equalised but it was one of those games where we just didn't perform.

"It ended up with them being awarded a penalty at the last minute from a rash challenge, Keith Gillespie got sent off. It was just a whole bundle of things that could go wrong did go wrong. I thought, 'We don't need to be losing here to Malta before we come

back to play the next competitive games. We're gonna get a big time bashing from everybody.'

"I remember being in the dug out praying for Maik Taylor to save the penalty and he did.

"We were very fortunate to get out of there 1–1. We had a long chat in the dressing room afterwards and I said, 'Look what do you wanna do? Is this what you want? To spend games like this where we've been undisciplined, almost lost and we fully deserved that. We've got big games coming up now. Is this what you want to be about? It's your team, what do you want from your team? Although I might be manager the team is yours, you need to take responsibility for the team and the performance and the result and we can't have anything like this ever happen again.' And to be fair it didn't."

Paul Ferguson is from Bangor, County Down but now lives in Belfast, working for the *Sunday Life* newspaper. He covered almost every single match under Lawrie's term, missing only a couple of the World Cup qualifiers.

PAUL FERGUSON:

"The turning point in Lawrie's fortunes with the team was, I believe, in Malta. It was only a friendly but immediately after that game Lawrie locked the players in the changing room for a good 20, 25 minutes maybe half an hour berating them. The players usually, on a night after a match, would head out but all of them more or less stayed in the team hotel having a couple of beers and that was it. The next morning at the airport there were long faces, they were miserable looking. And I felt that, as Lawrie would sometimes say, was the kick up the backside that those players needed because that was really the start of the fantastic run that Lawrie enjoyed.

"After it came the wins over Azerbaijan and England; we got beat by Wales and Austria but we were better than them, we actually performed very well and deserved to win those games, I would see those games as positives. Then we drew against Portugal – brilliant result against one of the top teams in the world – beat

ABOVE: Keith Gillespie can't believe he has been given a red card in the friendly match against Malta at the national stadium in Valletta.

BELOW: Lawrie and his backroom staff show their disappointment in the team performance against Malta.

Estonia, went on a very positive US tour where we found young players like Sammy Clingan, Kyle Lafferty and Steve Davis became the youngest ever captain, then there was Finland.

"Now the only one negative point in that 16 months was Iceland. For me it was the night when Lawrie Sanchez locked the changing room door in Valletta and gave them what for. That seemed to change their attitude."

8 WORLD CUP QUALIFYING GAMES
AZERBAIJAN AND ENGLAND

LAWRIE SANCHEZ:

"We had a good ten days. It started poorly in that two of the players, Phil Mulryne and Jeff Whitley were sent home for breach of team discipline which you wouldn't have wanted in the preparation for what were two crucial games. The two players let themselves down, let their team mates down and ultimately let the fans down. I had to take a very tough decision, certainly in Jeff's case because he would have played in those games and Mulryne would have been on the bench. To take that sort of action was the last thing I needed before what were going to be two crucial games for the team.

"But then again the sending home focused the team that we had to be professional and do things right."

IFA CHIEF EXECUTIVE HOWARD WELLS:

"Going on to win against Azerbaijan after the disappointing 1–1 draw with Malta in a friendly was important as when I arrived at the IFA in January 2005 I took the view that the last thing I wanted to be doing towards the end of that year was to be seeking a new manager. I have always felt, anyway, that international managers require two tournaments to prove themselves – one to learn about international football and the other to do something about it. I had encouraged the IFA to renew Lawrie's contract in March 2005, to allow me to focus on off-the-field problems. But ahead of the

OPPOSITE: The players and backroom staff celebrate their historic victory over England.

Azerbaijan and England matches, which were the turning point, there was 'chuntering' amongst a few within the IFA about 'who had renewed this man's contract.'"

3 SEPTEMBER 2005 – FIFA WORLD CUP 2006 QUALIFYING ROUNDS
NORTHERN IRELAND v AZERBAIJAN
WINDSOR PARK, BELFAST
RESULT: WIN 2–0
(STUART ELLIOTT, WARREN FEENEY)
ATTENDANCE: 11,909

This was the home win everyone had been waiting for – at last!!!

WARREN FEENEY:

"This was my first goal for Northern Ireland. My whole family was there and my wee girl, my first child, was born just the week before so it was great for me.

"It was a penalty and I wanted to be sure I was the first to get the ball to score the goal."

NI CAPTAIN AARON HUGHES:

"Azerbaijan was my first win, because I was injured during Estonia and I wasn't in the Caribbean.

ABOVE: Stuart can't hide his delight after scoring against Azerbaijan.

NI SUPPORTER ALAN FERRIS:

"Whenever the draw for the World Cup Qualifiers was made the date not only in my mind but naturally in the mind of every GAWA member was 7 September 2005 whenever OWC were to play host to England at Windsor Park. England have always been the best team in the British Isles and at that time had many, many world-class players, Beckham, Rooney, Lampard et al.

"A friend of mine who works at Newforge where Northern Ireland train, managed to sneak me in during one of the closed training sessions. Hidden behind a fence I watched and listened as Lawrie and his coaching staff put the players through their paces. The players listened attentively as Lawrie mentioned about Rooney making his runs from midfield, how Beckham's crosses would be accurate and how the English defence would double-up on our goal scoring machine Healy on every occasion.

"I was fearful but the players looked relaxed, Lawrie had instilled confidence into the team, the team believed, but the fans tried not to expect anything – but we could all dream."

ABOVE: Tony Capaldi during the Azerbaijan game at Windsor Park.

"I was ecstatic. Even though I hadn't been involved for various reasons in the other wins, I could see the positive effect it had on the lads and it was good to see them winning.

"Lawrie gave us the evening off to be with our families or go for a meal or whatever. So we all split up quite early in the evening. We didn't all get back together properly again until the next morning and it was great to just get up knowing you had won. It was a real feel good factor but to be honest it was forgotten about quite quickly because we had the England game coming up."

After Denise had left I was asked to stay longer, until the end of the World Cup qualifying campaign, and so I temporarily relinquished my other clients in England, absorbed her duties and worked full-time in Belfast. Preparing for the England match, particularly as it was a double header with Azerbaijan, was a huge job. We had the largest media contingent there had ever been for a game, with over 100 reporters and up to 40 photographers in addition to the huge BBC team televising the game live across the UK.

Fred McGee and Johnny McMeekin helped with the print journalists; distributing programmes, team sheets and overseeing the press box, while Dawn Smyth took charge of the Junior Supporter match mascots.

During the first half I stayed down on the touchline, by the corner where the players came in and out, standing with the BBC Northern Ireland (BBC NI) crew including reporter Mark Sidebottom and producer Rod Nawn.

I loved the atmosphere created by the fans, the continuous singing and waving of flags and the banners. I cannot listen to Neil Diamond's 'Sweet Caroline' without hearing in my head the Norn Iron version instead. And this was the time of 'Show me the way to Amarillo', so they were singing that too.

One of my favourite players was Keith, I had a soft spot for him because he had played for Newcastle United, the nearest big club to my childhood home in Northumberland. He was always very friendly, a gentlemen, often helped me with my suitcases at the airport and on the coach when we were travelling, as indeed did David [Healy]. I loved to watch him play because he was so committed and passionate about the shirt and often provided the passes which led to David scoring.

He always wore shirts with long sleeves and on the front, just around the neckline, there always appeared to be what looked like a massive wet stain. Eventually I asked Derek McKinley the kit man was on earth it was and he told me Keith plastered 'Vicks' all over his shirt prior to going out on the pitch to help with his breathing.

7 SEPTEMBER 2005 – FIFA WORLD CUP 2006 QUALIFYING ROUNDS
NORTHERN IRELAND v ENGLAND
WINDSOR PARK, BELFAST
RESULT: WIN 1–0
(DAVID HEALY)
ATTENDANCE: 14,069

ABOVE: Northern Ireland captain Aaron Hughes shakes hands with England captain David Beckham prior to kick-off at Windsor Park.

NI SUPPORTER ALAN FERRIS:

"The morning of the game, four of us in the office arrived with kit bags with our Northern Ireland shirts and scarves, we had a Northern Ireland CD playing from 8.30a.m. At nine o'clock two colleagues from a sister company in England arrived for a meeting, one had been here before and the other hadn't. The latter was confused, bemused and unclear of how the day would unfold. For reasons unknown (not) our meeting ended quicker than anticipated. At 11a.m. our guests were spirited away to a local hostelry where we joined the hoards of the GAWA. Neither of these gentlemen had tickets for the game but were determined to enjoy the occasion as much as us. One of them purchased a Northern Ireland shirt in Belfast before joining the Bangor Northern Ireland Supporters Club in a Chinese restaurant for what is now a pre-match ritual. This was washed down suitably and we headed up to the ground with hundreds of English and Northern Irish fans.

"My English friends wanted to get to the ground, buy a programme and savour the atmosphere before moving to a local pub to watch the match on TV. I won't go into the exact details of how I got two tickets outside the ground but needless to say my two friends joined us in the Kop and were part of an amazing night in Northern Irish football folklore.

"Celebrations continued until the early hours of Thursday morning – I made it to work on Monday!"

LAWRIE SANCHEZ:

"The England game was the turning point in many respects with what we were attempting to achieve with Northern Ireland. The fact that we got something, we actually won the game, meant that everything we had worked towards brought belief into the squad.

"I said to the players, 'This is a gimme for you, nobody expects us to win so whatever you do achieve will be held in high esteem.'

"We had a game plan and I brought in Les Reed to have a look at what we did, not just for the England game but to give us an oversight of what we needed to do. He had worked in the England camp with the national side and we wanted to make sure

that we were well prepared. He gave us some insight into what England do. He didn't have much interaction with the squad beyond observing but he did say at one meeting, 'If you do what I've seen you do over the course of this week you will cause England problems.' And I think after that one or two of the players, who had been a bit worried about it, relaxed."

IFA HEAD OF OPERATIONS WILLIAM CAMPBELL:

"My favourite memory of Lawrie's years is Northern Ireland 1 England 0.

"I came into the office on the morning of the England game at about eight o'clock to prepare for the security meeting and there were people going to their work in Northern Ireland shirts.

"Kick-off was 7.45p.m. Everyone was in the ground by 7.30p.m. Normally there's still queues until five minutes after kick-off. But everybody in the country knew that this was something big, a big event and everybody was there early for a special day. From early on you could see it, and I hadn't experienced that in a long, long time with the IFA.'

There was a frisson in the air that night. As the teams lined up in the tunnel area at the corner of Windsor Park several players held the hand of a Junior Supporter. Our boys, David Healy, Steve Davis, Keith Gillespie and Maik Taylor stood alongside the likes of Michael Owen, Steven Gerrard, Frank Lampard and Rio Ferdinand. The two captains, Aaron Hughes and David Beckham led their men out onto the pitch and from the first whistle it took on a dreamlike quality. The Northern Ireland supporters never stopped singing and when Wayne Rooney made his way off at half time he cast a moody glance in the direction of the Kop Stand. I felt like telling him it was nothing personal and that the Green and White Army were as vocal as this for every match.

NI CAPTAIN AARON HUGHES:

"I thought we could beat England. Knowing how much everyone wanted to play in it at the time, the build up to the game, the atmosphere at Windsor, and I thought if we set off right from the

ABOVE: Keith Gillespie tackles England's Wayne Rooney.

ABOVE: Ivan Sproule came on as a substitute towards the end of the match and is seen here with England's Ashley Cole.

start and do the things that Lawrie's telling us to do and stick to that game plan you never know what can happen."

STEPHEN CRAIGAN:

"At half time someone said to Lawrie in the dressing room that it was hard work chasing the ball and running about with little success and Lawrie said, 'It's hard work if you want to be a hero.' That has stuck with me and boy was he right."

In the second half when David sent his stunning shot past 'keeper Paul Robinson into the net and the stadium erupted I remember being picked up and swung around by Keith Tipping, the BT engineer who sets up the lines in the press box. William Campbell was pacing about with the biggest grin on his face and we were all biting our nails just wishing the final whistle would blow.

IFA HEAD OF OPERATIONS WILLIAM CAMPBELL:

"My best memory of the match was the realisation with three or four minutes of extra time to go that we were going to win. Because even when we scored there was still 15 or 16 minutes to go and you always felt that one of the top English player's Beckham or someone, would pitch a goal and the glorious win would be a glorious draw but maybe with a thought of what might have been.

"But after we got into time added on it was quite clear that England weren't going to score and that we were going to win. And there was a great feeling of elation and excitement and being a part of something very historic.

ABOVE: David Healy delivers a dream for the whole country.
BELOW: Keith Gillespie and David Healy celebrate the winning goal.

"People say Spain was the better game of football and it probably was but for me beating England was best. They were the big rivals with all the players that everybody knows and they came with such a big reputation and the fact that Northern Ireland had not beaten them in Belfast for such a long time, that was very special.

"Even now, if I'm feeling down I just go to the video and turn it on and I enjoy Healy's goal and the atmosphere."

NI SUPPORTER ALAN FERRIS:

"Those last 17 minutes were breathtaking, the noise inside Windsor was deafening. I looked over to the bench and saw Lawrie desperately attempting to bark out his instructions. The noise levels made this almost impossible, I had dreamt of a draw and after Healy scored I was choked. I held my nine-year-old daughter Emily as the tears of joy ran down my face whenever the referee finally blew the whistle. Lawrie and the team had given us the best night in Northern Ireland football in over 20 years and I was there!"

NI CAPTAIN AARON HUGHES:

"I think the England game has to be my favourite match. We've had some great results, even after that possibly more important results with regards the standing in the table, but the pure emotion of the game and the atmosphere can't be beaten. I can always remember, the thing that sticks in my head, at the final whistle you normally get a big cheer from the crowd but it was totally different. It was almost like a scream, you could hear the excitement in everyone's voice. We'd beaten England and the place went mad. It's probably up there as the best moment in my footballing career so far."

JAMES QUINN:

"Without a shadow of a doubt the one that meant the most to me was the England win because it was our first real biggy. I had missed the away tie at Old Trafford due to suspension and I was heartbroken. I wanted revenge for the 4–0.

"It was the greatest night of my life even outside football, nothing comes close. I still sit down now with my dad and we watch it and go through it and we joke, 'Oh we're gonna get beat 3–0 here.'

"It wasn't a fluke, we outfought them and we got what we deserved. And that's why we went on to beat Spain and Sweden and got to top of the group [during the UEFA Euro 2008 qualifying tournament].

"Straight after the game as the whistle went I turned and saw Frank Lampard standing there and I asked for his shirt and he was as good as gold, very kind. He said, 'Congratulations, you deserved that, enjoy your evening, fair play to you,' and he gave me his top.

"I'm not sure the rest of the England team were so cool about it but stuff them, they were going back to a 100 grand a week. I was going back to Peterborough United to play Grimsby away on Saturday."

Kate Hoey MP was sitting in the director's box alongside Lawrie's partner Claire. They had known one another from some years previously when Claire worked for the Professional Footballers' Association and Kate was educational advisor at several high-profile English football clubs.

KATE HOEY MP:

"I was delighted when I met Claire again and we tended to sit together for most of the matches. When she first came to Northern Ireland I knew lots of people there and she didn't so it was nice to be able to introduce her.

"In the director's box everyone stands when there is a goal scored. Claire and I were sitting in the third row on the left hand side of the box right behind the English FA, Trevor Brooking, Geoff Thompson (chief executive) and the whole of the FA party. We were screeching and screaming throughout the match but when it got to the last four minutes we were just awful. I remember afterwards Claire apologising to one of the FA board that we had probably deafened him but he said he understood. Trevor Brooking was particularly good that night because he was the only one of the English FA party that really knew what it meant to the supporters and all of us, and he was very generous in his praise of our supporters and team whereas the rest of them couldn't get on their jet plane quick enough. Except for David Beckham, he was wonderful.

"He made a point when he came out of going behind the bus to sign autographs, and he had clapped our supporters before he left the pitch whereas the others all kept their heads down. I think David Beckham is a true professional."

IFA CHIEF EXECUTIVE HOWARD WELLS:

"The FA contingent including the chairman Geoff Thompson and Brian Barwick were very gracious in defeat as they were at the 125th anniversary dinner (in November) when the subject was raised many times, and eventually they waved their white napkins in the air! They took the result on the chin as all good professionals do."

And indeed, I found that to be the case too. As I waited for Lawrie to emerge from the bunker room to do his post-match press conference Adrian Bevington, the FA's Head (now Director) of Communications, was waiting outside the England dressing room and congratulated me warmly.

Lawrie, as always, was the coolest operator in the whole stadium. When, in later days, there were problems with the media and they complained about what they perceived to be arrogance I reminded them about Lawrie's reaction to the England game. In victory as in defeat, his demeanour never altered and at the post-match press conference, which was now being held in the Bass Lounge, while all other faces were wreathed in smiles his was composed.

Of course Lawrie was overjoyed with the win, but he applies the principals of Rudyard Kipling's inspirational and motivational poem *If* in his approach to life.

ABOVE: Maik Taylor shows his delight and relief at the end of the match.

IF

by Rudyard Kipling

If you can keep your head when all about you
Are losing theirs and blaming it on you,
If you can trust yourself when all men doubt you,
But make allowance for their doubting too;
If you can wait and not be tired by waiting,
Or being lied about, don't deal in lies,
Or being hated, don't give way to hating,
And yet don't look too good, nor talk too wise:
If you can dream – and not make dreams your master,
If you can think – and not make thoughts your aim;
If you can meet with Triumph and Disaster
And treat those two impostors just the same;
If you can bear to hear the truth you've spoken
Twisted by knaves to make a trap for fools,
Or watch the things you gave your life to, broken,
And stoop and build 'em up with worn-out tools:
If you can make one heap of all your winnings
And risk it all on one turn of pitch-and-toss,
And lose, and start again at your beginnings
And never breath a word about your loss;
If you can force your heart and nerve and sinew
To serve your turn long after they are gone,
And so hold on when there is nothing in you
Except the Will which says to them: "Hold on!"
If you can talk with crowds and keep your virtue,
Or walk with kings – nor lose the common touch,
If neither foes nor loving friends can hurt you,
If all men count with you, but none too much;
If you can fill the unforgiving minute
With sixty seconds' worth of distance run,
Yours is the Earth and everything that's in it,
And – which is more – you'll be a Man, my son!
Rudyard Kipling (1865–1936)

Lines from the poem appear over the player's entrance to Wimbledon Tennis Club's centre court and the mottos and maxims for life contained within it have been used by many sportsmen as a blueprint for personal integrity, behaviour and self-development.

LAWRIE SANCHEZ:

"It was a fantastic night. That for me was a turning point with what we could achieve with Northern Ireland.

"The Kipling poem If says that if you win or lose you should treat both impostors the same and that's how I deal with it.

"I was pleased that we had done a professional job, pleased for the players. There is a paternal pride when you are a manager. And I was pleased for the fans as well.

"It was nearly 80 years since England had been beaten in Belfast and to be in a competitive fixture too made it even better.

"Sometimes sport transcends politics and I think on that night it did for Northern Ireland."

FORMER IFA PRESS OFFICER DENISE WARD:

"I watched the England game in the September on television at home and I was absolutely gutted whenever Healy scored the goal and I wasn't there to be part of it. I was quite emotional.

"I was invited to the match but I just thought it would be too painful to go and sit there as a guest without a proper role to play. My former colleagues would have been busy working, and all the faces were changing at the IFA, and I wouldn't have been involved. Perhaps with hindsight now, I should have gone."

NI SPORTS MASSAGE THERAPIST PAUL PRENTICE:

"Being a Northern Ireland fan it was a massive honour to be there as part of the team, and very, very exciting to watch the match and the result just complimented the whole game. I believe it was the turning point in Northern Ireland football at international and local level. It used to be years ago that everywhere you looked kids were wearing Manchester United, Liverpool, Rangers or Celtic jerseys whereas now everywhere you look they're wearing Northern Ireland jerseys. I think it really helped to promote the sport over here.

"Being part of the atmosphere and the squad that night, the most memorable thing was walking around the pitch after the game singing, 'We're not Brazil, we're Northern Ireland,' to all the fans and having the scarves thrown at us. It was just an unbelievable experience that I'll never forget."

NI FAN STEPHEN ALEXANDER:

"There is a very loyal core of Northern Ireland fans who basically sing through everything. They are a credit to themselves, to the team and to their country. In sectarian times they were being over-shadowed by a minority, but this particular group have always been a credit and have tried to create a good atmosphere at home matches. They are really just a fantastic bunch of supporters, as was later proved when they won the award for the Best Supporters in Europe in 2006."

I was relieved to later learn from several Northern Ireland supporters that the English fans behaved impeccably and took the defeat in good heart. One guy told me about a group of English fans who had brought cigars over to smoke after the game, expecting to savour victory. In the event they handed their cigars over to the Northern Ireland supporters and shared a celebratory drink.

After the match I joined Howard Wells, Roy Millar (IFA director of coaching) and their wives at The Wellington Park Hotel where we watched the game being re-played by BBC NI on a huge screen to the delight of the mass of supporters packed into the lounge.

NI CAPTAIN AARON HUGHES:

"After the game, with my wife Samantha and my brother and sister, we went back to my best friend Steve's house to get changed and we went out for a drink to celebrate the win. Steve's a hockey player and we used to play hockey together when I was younger. Then we had some pizza."

And in all of this madness, while the car horns were tooting turning the centre of Belfast into Buenos Aires, as highly-regarded Northern Ireland journalist Dr Malcolm Brodie famously reported, and the fans were singing long into the night, the country delirious with joy, where was the star of the show, Mr David Healy, uncrowned king of Northern Ireland? His low-key celebration sums up what the Northern Ireland squad is all about and why perhaps so many of us who were lucky enough to work with these down to earth young men regarded it as one of the greatest privileges in our careers.

DAVID HEALY:

"You can always dream, especially as a boy growing up, that something big will happen and on that night something big did happen. We were organised and up for it and we probably deserved our win.

"At the time we were expected to go out and as we did at Old Trafford, crumble and get beaten 4–0 but by this time the boys had a lot more belief in where we wanted to go. And listening to what Lawrie said after the game, he said before it he had five or six players believing we were gonna get a result and by half time he had the whole eleven, the whole crowd and everybody with anything to do with Norn Ireland believing that we could get an unbelievable result.

"Full credit to Lawrie, he never made a negative substitution on the night. It would have been easy to settle for a 0–0 draw but he stuck at it and we ground it out.

"I celebrated in my hotel room. I had a chicken sandwich and a blackcurrant and lemonade. Quite a few of the lads go out on occasions after the games but for whatever reason on this night nobody wanted to. I think we were all just emotionally drained. I got a lift back to the hotel from my parents and I lay on the bed to watch the football over a pint of blackcurrant and lemonade."

Class.

9 WORLD CUP QUALIFYING GAMES
WALES AND AUSTRIA

8 OCTOBER 2005 – FIFA WORLD CUP 2006
QUALIFYING ROUNDS
NORTHERN IRELAND v WALES
WINDSOR PARK, BELFAST
RESULT: LOST 3–2
(KEITH GILLESPIE, STEVE DAVIS)
ATTENDANCE: 13,451

KEITH GILLESPIE:

"Scoring was a big thing for me because I had scored my first goal for Northern Ireland 11 years before. For me to go 11 years without scoring for my country is a long time. It was nice that it was at Windsor Park. The only downside was that we lost the game. As far as playing for your country goes it's the end result that matters, it doesn't matter who scores."

12 OCTOBER 2005 – FIFA WORLD CUP 2006
QUALIFYING ROUNDS
AUSTRIA v NORTHERN IRELAND
ERNST HAPPEL STADIUM, VIENNA
RESULT: LOST 2–0
ATTENDANCE: 12,500

ABOVE: Northern Ireland backroom staff in the dug out prior to the Wales game. From the left: Dave Beasant, Terry Gibson, Terry Hayes, Doc and Paul Prentice.
OPPOSITE: A new fan joins the ranks of the GAWA in Vienna.

NI SUPPORTER ALAN FERRIS:

"Another memorable night was whenever 1,500 members of the GAWA stayed behind in Vienna for 30 minutes to show our support for Lawrie and the team. This was reciprocated by Lawrie addressing the fans over the stadium PA system. He was genuine in his praises and in his words of gratitude to his fans. We were grateful and had a real belief that Lawrie was taking us in the right direction. He had demonstrated an ability to be firm with those who did not abide with his plans and decisions à la Whitley and Mulryne. He had

ABOVE LEFT: The manager training in Vienna.

RIGHT: Colin Murdock and Michael Duff work together to take control in Austria.

dropped one of my favourite players Keith Gillespie early on. But that in my opinion was the restoration of Keith's career. Keith returned to the team as a very early substitute in Baku against Azerbaijan in October 2004 and the 80 plus fans on that away trip were happy to see him return. From that game on Gillespie has been magnificent for us.

"The feel good factor amongst the fans was amazing. I had sat in the stands and stood in the terracing for years witnessing below average, and that is being generous, performances, but following Lawrie's appointment the performance by the players was there to be seen. Lawrie had achieved all his goals and I for one was delighted and very impressed."

ABOVE: The Northern Ireland fans collecting in the centre of Vienna on match day prior to their traditional march to the stadium.

ABOVE: The GAWA in full voice at the Ernst Happel Stadium in Vienna.

RIGHT: Damien Johnson takes the ball from Austria's Markus Kiesenebner.

LAWRIE SANCHEZ:

"We played very, very well that night but ultimately got undone. I thought it was a very unfair result.

"It was marred by Damien Johnson getting sent off, which was going to come back and affect us because he'd miss the first three games of the next campaign because of violent conduct.

"I remember the fans that night, 3,000 in Vienna, I went across to address them because the stadium manager asked me, 'Why don't your fans go home?'

"And I said, 'Because they're here and they wanna enjoy it, we played well, it's the end of the campaign, we finished fourth. We had been in the bottom two of the group but we finished above Wales and Azerbaijan and we've beaten England and they just want to enjoy the night.'

"So he said, 'Well will you tell them to go home?'

"And I went across to the fans and I remember saying to them, 'Thanks for your support, fantastic support. We'll do better next time.'"

At the end of the World Cup campaign Lawrie's assistant manager, World Cup hero Gerry Armstrong amicably decided to leave the backroom staff. His wife was due to have their baby in September. With his property business and SKY commitments he didn't want to spend so much time travelling away from his family.

Northern Ireland had started the tournament seeded fifth in Group Six, with only Azerbaijan below and finished fourth behind England, Poland and Austria.

Northern Ireland had punched above the expected weight, but the biggest surprises were yet to come.

ABOVE: Lawrie discusses tactics with Terry Gibson and kit man Derek McKinley.

10 125TH ANNIVERSARY DINNER AND PORTUGAL FRIENDLY

ABOVE: Lawrie Sanchez with his partner Claire Weir at the Irish Football Association 125th anniversary dinner held at Belfast City Hall.
OPPOSITE: Grant McCann making a run for possession in the friendly match against Portugal.

ABOVE: Alex Steele (co-founder of the Amalgamation of Northern Ireland Supporters Clubs); Dickie Best, father of George; and eminent Northern Ireland journalist Dr Malcolm Brodie.

In November a magnificent banquet for over 400 guests including delegates from FIFA and UEFA, plus associations from around Europe was held at Belfast City Hall.

The glittering event, held to celebrate the 125th anniversary of the Irish Football Association, was organised by IFA honorary treasurer David Martin and his committee.

A book, compiled and edited by Dr Malcolm Brodie and Billy Kennedy was published for the occasion with messages of support from FIFA

President Joseph Sepp Blatter and UEFA President Lennart Johansson.

On the night every guest received a copy of the book, gentleman also received a watch and ladies a bracelet. Lawrie and his partner Claire, players, IFA executive committee members and staff, media and supporters were amongst the guests.

The banquet was a glorious celebration of football in the province and something of which to be justly proud. Players past and present were inducted into the Nationwide-sponsored IFA Hall of Fame. Warm wishes were sent to George Best, at that time seriously ill in a London hospital and very near to death. Peter Corry sang and everyone feasted on a meal of Ulster beef, Bushmills sauce, traditional champ and Armagh apple lattice tartlet.

ABOVE: UTV team: The beautiful Claire McCullom with Adrian Logan (left) and Neil Brittain (right).
BELOW: Some of the BBC NI team with friends. From the left: legendary commentator and presenter Jackie Fullerton; John O'Neill; unknown guest; Karen Bowen, wife of the former IFA general secretary David Bowen; former sports editor Ed Smith, former Head of Sport Terry Smyth.

ABOVE: Northern Ireland football writers Mark McIntosh (left) and Paul Ferguson (right), with photographer William Cherry in the centre.

15 NOVEMBER 2005 – INTERNATIONAL FRIENDLY MATCH
NORTHERN IRELAND v PORTUGAL
WINDSOR PARK, BELFAST
RESULT: DRAW 1–1
(WARREN FEENEY)
ATTENDANCE: 14,000

LAWRIE SANCHEZ:

"Felipe Scolari brought a very good side including Ronaldo.

"Again with friendlies we had a weakened team but I remember we played excellent that night. Steve Davis and Chris Brunt were excellent in the centre of midfield, two young kids.

"We proved that we could compete with the best even though we had a weakened team."

WARREN FEENEY:

"Lawrie gave me a start that night because I think David was injured. There were a lot of injuries, but it was a good game to be involved in and I scored a header so I was quite pleased to get another goal."

NI COACH TERRY GIBSON:

"Those games were quite easy for us to be honest because although it was a friendly it was a glamorous match to be involved in and we had a good turn-out from the squad. I think we had one or two missing. It's easy to motivate the players because they want to take part in a game like that. There was never any doubt that as long as they were fit they were going to be there.

"It was a big thrill and a great result for us. I remember us playing our usual aggressive game which upset one or two of the Portuguese players and in particular upset the bench. I think they thought that because it was a friendly we should have gone easy on them a little bit in terms of how we played, but for our players, and all of us involved, it was a game we felt we could get something from because we were making progress and to pick up a scalp like Portugal was a big incentive to us.

"We approached it in the right way. We had Chris Brunt and Steve Davis in the centre of midfield and Warren Feeney scored the goal, a header. It was great for us to get the draw."

BELOW: Warren Feeney later went on to score a header resulting in a draw for Northern Ireland against Portugal.

ABOVE: Steve Jones, Stephen Craigan and Tony Capaldi take on Portugal's Cristiano Ronaldo.

"Ronaldo showed his class throughout the game, it was evident that he was a top, top player, he was the main attraction. He was used to the British style of football, it was one or two of the other players who weren't used to it. We work hard at closing people down and getting tackles in and things like that, and we upset one or two and upset the bench as well.

"Phil Scolari is like a big, tough grisly bear but he didn't like us getting stuck into his precious players. He was quite critical after the game, but what did he expect? He was manager of Brazil and won the World Cup, he was manager of a fantastic team with Portugal and little Northern Ireland fancied their chances of doing well again. We certainly weren't going to sit back and let them play us off the pitch and embarrass ourselves. So we played our usual game and it was good to hear him moaning at the end because I think there's nothing worse for a manager or a coach to have the manager or coach from the other team patronising you after you've been beaten. I've got great respect for Scolari and the fact that he was moaning after the game meant that we had done our job and achieved something."

My work with the IFA was completed after the Portugal game.

Back home in England I watched news bulletins about the failing health of George Best, spotting in the footage some of the Northern Ireland media outside the hospital where he lay. When he died on Friday 25 November I interviewed IFA president Jim Boyce and on the instruction of Howard Wells sent out a press release from the IFA.

ABOVE: Ivan Sproule wins the ball.

11 FRIENDLIES AND THE USA TOUR

1 MARCH 2006 – INTERNATIONAL
FRIENDLY MATCH
NORTHERN IRELAND v ESTONIA
WINDSOR PARK, BELFAST
RESULT: WIN 1–0
(IVAN SPROULE)
ATTENDANCE: 14,000

ABOVE: Wrapped up against the cold to face Estonia in a friendly at Windsor.
OPPOSITE: Alan Mannus in America.

NI COACH TERRY GIBSON:

"It was a very wintry night in Belfast, not a glamorous game but what amazed me was we still had a 14,000 sell out in the stadium.

"The supporters appreciated what they were seeing from the players and over a period of time our matches became events and people wanted to be there, whether it was playing Portugal or Estonia on a snowy night. If it had been a competitive match it might have been abandoned and it was just amazing that we had a sell-out crowd again and they got behind us. We never had a match at Windsor where it was half empty and it was difficult to motivate the players. Whenever the players turned up and we got to Windsor Park and there was a sell-out crowd that got behind you there was no way that the players couldn't give 100 per cent. We've got a lot to be thankful for there because there's nothing worse than trying to motivate players in a half empty stadium and generally people not caring. But over the three years that we had, we were fortunate in that we got a head of steam up and the

supporters wanted to be involved in every occasion that we had. We're different to a club team in that we don't play every week and they don't get the chance to see us every fortnight, it was every couple of months and they made the most of it when the international team was in town and it was just always a great occasion.

"It was good to get a win again. We were getting used to getting results and we didn't want to let them slip. Ivan's goal came early in the game. It was terrific for him, he hadn't been in the squad many times before, he was just breaking into it, and that cemented his place in Lawrie's thinking that he was a player of great potential. Everyone knows he's got fantastic speed."

RIGHT: Steve Davis playing in the snow against Estonia at Windsor Park.

BELOW: Ivan Sproule scores the winner on a wintry night in Belfast.

TRIP TO THE USA:
TWO INTERNATIONAL
FRIENDLY AWAY MATCHES
21 MAY 2006 –

v URUGUAY in NEW JERSEY
LOST 1–0
26 MAY 2006 –

v ROMANIA in CHICAGO
LOST 2–0

NI COACH TERRY GIBSON:

"It was the end of the season and some players were involved in play-off's and there's always players who have to have minor surgery to deal with injuries that they've been playing with during the season, so we had a lot of dropouts, but it gave us the chance to bring in some younger players to have a look at.

"On that trip we had some of the best training sessions that we'd ever had, every single player gave every session 100 per cent. It was a very young squad, we had some older heads in there like Colin Murdock and Stephen Craigan who helped them along the way. Everyone was full of enthusiasm, these youngsters who were so thrilled to be away representing their country. We were in an exciting place, New York and Chicago, and we had two great games to look forward to and fantastic stadiums. We played in the Giant's Stadium and the home of the Chicago Bears and I can remember all the players taking pictures in the stadium beforehand on the pitch and we weren't used to the size of the changing rooms. It was just a completely different experience and I think we got everything we could out of that trip.

"It made it slightly easier for us in terms of discipline because most of them were under the age of 21 and couldn't get served a drink so it had its benefits.

"We didn't get any wins on that tour but it was well worth the trip. Steve Davis was captain which I think will help him in the long run and we had Kyle Lafferty and Sammy Clingan come into the squad and really create a good impression. And we also had Jeff Hughes, Dean Shiels, Mark Hughes and they all created a really good impression and of course Kyle and Sammy kept their places in the squad. And that's what makes those trips worthwhile."

ABOVE: Lawrie with Linfield's Peter Thompson prior to the US tour.

ABOVE: Arriving in America at the start of the US Tour. Lawrie at the team hotel in New Jersey with Kyle Lafferty, a new addition to the squad.

NI SPORTS MASSAGE THERAPIST PAUL PRENTICE:

"The majority of my work is in the treatment room with Terry [Hayes], but whenever we are travelling I help Derek [McKinley, the kit man] quite a bit with all the equipment through airports and on coaches.

"The best trip for me personally was the tour to America. I was able to bond quite a bit with some of the players that I hadn't already bonded with and at the same time I got to know a lot of the younger players coming through, the likes of Kyle Lafferty, Sammy Clingan, Sean Webb. So it was good for me on a professional level to work with a different variety of players, because when you are with the same

bunch of guys over and over again you do get to know what they like, what they don't like, what they are prone to injury wise.

"There is one particular player who has one of the highest pain thresholds that I've ever come across when I am treating someone and that is Damien Johnson. It doesn't matter how hard you go on a treatment or how deep into the muscle you go he just lies there and if you wanna go harder he says, 'Yeah, not a problem.' Whereas there are certain boys who if you put your hand on them they're jumping off the bed."

For years the Northern Ireland media had travelled and stayed with the team on away fixtures. But the USA tour was to be the last time this happened.

NI JOURNALIST PAUL FERGUSON:

"Myself and [Dr] Malcolm Brodie were the only print journalists on that US tour, Jackie Fullerton was there for television and there were two photographers. That was the only media.

"I wrote a piece on the Sunday morning ahead of the Uruguay game. It was a money story basically saying that the IFA, even though they had said they were going to make a decent amount of money out of this tour were actually only going to break about even; and there was a line in it about players' pocket money and an unnamed player quoted.

"The players were supposed to get pocket money and at the time I went to print on the Saturday night they hadn't been paid this pocket money. Some of the players were disgruntled that they had not received this money. They subsequently received it on the Sunday I'm led to believe. It was a throw-away line at the end of a back-page story.

"Lawrie seemed to take objection to this piece, as did certain members of the IFA. Now the only person who spoke to me about this afterwards was Jim Boyce and we had words and he wanted to know why I'd run the story, and then that seemed to be it.

"Lawrie said if I hadn't spoken to a player in the team hotel I wouldn't have got the story. A couple of months later he subsequently agreed I would have got the story because of my

ABOVE: Sammy Clingan in America.

contacts with the players, so it didn't matter that I was staying in the team hotel. But David Segel [of West End Travel] received a phone call from Howard when we were in America saying that from now on the press were not permitted to stay with the team.

"But from what I gather, Lawrie had this in mind months before the US tour. I think having spoken to certain members of the English, Scottish and maybe Welsh FA he realised that this was not the way they conducted tours and they didn't have the media in the team hotel.

"The US tour was organised, he couldn't do anything about that, the media were there but from what I understand he'd wanted the media to stay at a different hotel for some time before that."

IFA TRAVEL AGENT DAVID SEGEL:

"I received an email from Howard Wells, not a phone call, informing me that after discussing the matter with Lawrie Sanchez it had

ABOVE: Northern Ireland v Uruguay International Challenge Match held at The Giants Stadium, New York. Lawrie with his backroom team and some of the squad.
RIGHT: Lawrie at the Northern Ireland training ground, University of Illinois, Chicago.

been decided that the press would in future no longer be permitted to stay in the same hotel as the team party."

LAWRIE SANCHEZ:

"There had been discussions within the IFA from when I first took over the Northern Ireland job about moving the press out of the team hotel, but everyone was wary about when and how to do it because they knew it would cause problems. But it was unusual in the modern day for the press to share hotels with teams.

"The argument in Northern Ireland was that we were a small country and we had always done it and that was the way it was. I had a discussion with David Bowen when I first came in and was asked if they should move the press from the team hotel, and I said

ABOVE: Ivan Sproule on the US tour in the match against Romania.

LEFT: Northern Ireland's Gareth McAuley.

to leave it for the time being. It was a discussion that was raised again when Howard took over and the decision was to do it, the only question being when?

"The general consensus was that it would be after the summer at the start of the new campaign.

"Paul did a story that was ultimately wrong. Howard and Jim were very annoyed with it, as I was. And part of the argument was if he hadn't been in the hotel and talking to the players on an off-the-record basis the story might never have been written. But that

wasn't the reason the press were not allowed to share the team hotel in future, it was the catalyst to believing this was the right time to make that decision.

"It was based on no other reason than that in the modern era it is unusual to have an international team sharing a hotel with their press. The players like their privacy when they are away with the team and they don't want to feel that with press men in the room every other conversation they are having might be overheard. The press would say that anything heard in those circumstances would never be reported.

"The decision was made that from the next campaign it would be different, and this was put to the press in the best possible way, no slight was intended, it was just that the team wanted privacy and *it was the general way things were going in the football world.*

"But obviously with the long association some of the press had with the Northern Ireland team they took it as a slight and ultimately probably used it as a reason for a change in their reporting, certainly in regard to myself for having the audacity to do it."

NI JOURNALIST PAUL FERGUSON:

"We [the Northern Ireland football media] had a couple of meetings later during the summer with Lawrie where he put his views across saying we were boom-and-bust journalists, when things were going right everything was wonderful and if a slight thing went wrong we were doom merchants. We disagreed with this and said that we were reporting the facts and giving an honest opinion and nothing else."

LAWRIE SANCHEZ:

"Prior to the Finland game and before the European campaign Howard and I had a couple of off-the-record, no-holds-barred, meetings with the media. I told them the hotel decision had not been mine alone, it had come from the top but I had agreed to it. There was a lot of whinging about it. I said there was no slight intended against them, the team needed privacy and they didn't want their conversations overheard at breakfast. I said everything would be done to give them access on a professional basis at press conferences and open training. But I said, 'We are a small team, we'll have our big nights, we'll have our bad nights, there's the good feel factor which the media were an intimate part of, try not to do boom-and-bust reporting.'"

PHOTOGRAPHER WILLIAM CHERRY:

"At first I didn't like the idea of change, of having the media in a different hotel, but after a few games I quite liked not being under the feet of the players and staff. It's better for the players I think – they can relax without the journalists being there 24/7.

"On the trip to Finland, myself and Paul Ferguson from the Sunday Life were making our own way to our hotel; this was the first away trip the press and the team were in separate hotels. We weren't sure what the parameters would be – would we be allowed to photograph the players at their hotel? When we got to the airport we recognised some of the IFA crates; they'd obviously been delayed and hadn't arrived with the team and staff. I rang Lawrie who was already at the hotel and he said the crates contained the team kit and he asked if we could bring them with us, but they wouldn't fit in the taxi! So we organised a van. When we got to the hotel, Lawrie said he owed us one and so we were allowed to take pictures at the hotel after all."

16 AUGUST 2006 – INTERNATIONAL FRIENDLY MATCH
FINLAND v NORTHERN IRELAND
OLYMPIC STADIUM, HELSINKI
RESULT: WIN 2–1
(DAVID HEALY, KYLE LAFFERTY)
ATTENDANCE: 4,500

LAWRIE SANCHEZ:

"We beat Finland very comfortably with a good performance and everything seemed to be okay until we came to Iceland."

NI JOURNALIST PAUL FERGUSON:

"To be honest I had no problem with changing the hotel. The first time I experienced the change of hotel was in Finland. At the end of the day all I wanted from Lawrie Sanchez and the players was to conduct professional interviews with them as laid out in the itinerary.

"We went to Finland, had a great result, the players chatted away, did their interviews, Lawrie spoke at length. Everybody was gearing up for the Iceland match. Lawrie did say, 'Don't hype this up too much, if we lose I'll carry the can.'

"And then we played Iceland."

ABOVE: Lawrie, his backroom staff and the squad training in Helsinki prior to beating Finland 2–1.

RIGHT: Lawrie at training talking to Roy Hodgson, the Finnish manager.

IFA HEAD OF INTERNATIONAL ADMINISTRATION DAVID CURRIE:

"I think it probably is a good idea to have separate hotels because the players need a bit of space and previously they were getting stopped as they came down for dinner. They need their space."

UEFA EURO 2008 QUALIFYING GAMES

ICELAND AND SPAIN

In September the UEFA Euro 2008 qualifying tournament began with two home games at Windsor Park both of which would create headlines, but for quite different reasons.

Jon Goodman, a former striker with the Republic of Ireland, had known Lawrie at Wimbledon and joined the Northern Ireland backroom team as conditioning coach, a role he also held at English Premiership club Reading.

JON GOODMAN:

"Lawrie really wanted me to focus very much on the smaller details of the daily training regime building up to the matches, and to ensure best practices were implemented to ensure maximum recovery following matches. The recovery aspect was particularly important as the second match was always four days after the first. Looking back, I think we were successful every midweek match following the Saturday.

"It's a difficult position as the players are not 'owned' by Northern Ireland and therefore I have to respect that they may be given different information from the conditioners at their clubs. It was a case of evolution rather than revolution.

"We would discuss the duration and intensity of training every day to ensure we were physically prepared for the ensuing match. The nutrition and fluid intake was an essential part of ensuring players recovered rapidly between training and matches. The

players would take ice baths and recovery drinks following the matches to ensure maximum recovery.

"Also, a few guys that didn't play on the Saturday would need extra conditioning work to maintain their fitness levels. I would oversee this with the help of Terry Gibson and Dave Beasant."

2 SEPTEMBER 2006 – UEFA EURO 2008 QUALIFYING ROUNDS
NORTHERN IRELAND v ICELAND
WINDSOR PARK, BELFAST
RESULT: LOST 3–0
ATTENDANCE: 14,000

NI SUPPORTER ALAN FERRIS:

"A 3–0 home defeat against Iceland was a disastrous start. Some of the fans including myself booed, not the team, but the performance of the team after this result. I will always give 100 per cent to my country but I was disgusted and embarrassed at this result. I had two friends over from Newcastle for this game. I had told them how amazing the support was and how much improved our wee country were, I was devastated.

"Wednesday against Spain could not come quickly enough, we needed to bury this result and move on. We all realised we needed a result otherwise the competition was invariably over. Had Lawrie

OPPOSITE: Lawrie's farewell to the fans after the Spain match.

the motivating skills and tenacity to lift a deflated team to take on one of Europe's finest? We were about to find out."

LAWRIE SANCHEZ:

"I knew Iceland would be a very difficult game, they had more Premiership players than we did, and I knew how good they were. Unfortunately, the press wrote off Iceland who then came into Northern Ireland having read the stories about how straightforward a win it would be for us. One of their backroom staff said that was their team talk. Their manager said, 'You've read the press, they obviously don't take us seriously. Let's go out and show 'em.'

"Subsequently they got three goals in the first half, through poor defending. That said, we had something like 70 entries into their penalty box in the 90 minutes which was a phenomenal rate. But we lost 3–0 and it crystallised the press's annoyance at being out of the hotel, and antipathy towards myself and the team and they pretty much wrote us off: time for change, time for a new manager, the qualification was over already after game one. It was everything, but everything, that I had asked them not to do and from then on, for me, the chasm never closed again."

ABOVE: Lawrie at training prior to playing Iceland.

LEFT: Northern Ireland and Iceland take to the field at Windsor Park.

NI JOURNALIST PAUL FERGUSON:

"At the post-match press conference Lawrie said he was going to have a Sunday from hell, he wasn't going to enjoy reading the Sunday papers, this despite the fact that he had said on numerous occasions that he didn't read the papers. But he said he was ready for it.

"I can only speak for myself and my match report and comment pieces but I thought I was fair and accurate. And I stand by everything that I wrote. I can't speak for all my colleagues but for the majority of them I read their articles and I thought they were fair and just."

ABOVE: The team line-up before facing Iceland.

NI CAPTAIN AARON HUGHES:

"I thought things had got out of proportion a little bit. There was so much hype and excitement before the Iceland game and it felt like people got carried away afterwards. We'd played one game at the start of a campaign and already our campaign was over apparently. It was implied that we stood no chance of qualifying and it was back to the same old, same old.

"'I think that was harsh because it was one game and we still had eleven to go."

NI CONDITIONING COACH JON GOODMAN:

"At the time it was dreadful but my favourite memory is how we went from losing to Iceland 3–0 on the Saturday to beating Spain 3–2 on the Wednesday.

"As you can imagine, Lawrie was in a dark mood on the Sunday following the result and I was getting all sorts of texts from the Reading lads suggesting it was my fault! I got a phone call from Lawrie to come to a meeting with Terry G and Dave Beasant. We watched the video of the match and looked at some ProZone

analysis and realised we weren't as bad as the media would have us believe!

"We then set about developing a plan to beat Spain that ultimately resulted in that great night and a David Healy hat-trick.

"I was always interested in what went on at international level behind the scenes, and to experience it first hand was an honour. Lawrie was a great man to work for and was very communicative and supportive with the staff which made us all feel a part of the process.

"The beauty of club football is that there is always another match to focus on. When we lost a game at Reading we kept it in perspective as there are 38 matches over the course of the season."

ABOVE: Stephen Craigan in the Iceland game.

LEFT: Keith Gillespie in his trademark long-sleeved shirt covered in 'Vicks'.
ABOVE: Steve Davis getting knocked back from the ball.
BELOW: Sammy Clingan making a run in the Iceland game.

"The pressure on every international match was enormous.

"Lawrie and Steve [Coppell, manager of Reading] are similar in many ways, deep thinkers, honest with their players and meticulous in their planning and preparation. Probably the greatest difference would be in their relationship with their staff. Lawrie sought the opinion of us all on a daily basis whereas Steve tends to keep his thoughts to himself and entrust the staff to get on with their jobs independently.

"I would say that the Northern Ireland squad was unique in that the atmosphere and the players' approach to training were very similar to club football. The relationship the players had with some of the staff was very special too, especially with Derek the kit man who was loved by all!"

With the match over the team got back to their hotel and back to training on Monday morning. The following afternoon Lawrie held his regular pre-match press conference.

NI JOURNALIST PAUL FERGUSON:

"Prior to the Tuesday press conference starting we had a little pre-chat with Lawrie about certain things which had happened after Saturday's match. He had taken an age to come down to the post-match press conference and we were saying, 'Look we know you were defeated, you obviously had a lot of things to say to the players, but you were over an hour coming down to the press conference and we have deadlines to meet. Can we meet somewhere in the middle?'

"So from that he went on the defensive. It was as if the entire media conference was against him.

"Lawrie received a few tough questions which he didn't like. He was asked by a correspondent from England whether he would consider his position if we got beat by Spain. Immediately he said, 'No comment. Next question.' But this question had obviously hit a nerve, he was visibly shaken by it and you could see that it rattled him and he was completely on the defensive."

LAWRIE SANCHEZ:

"I was asked in the press conference, 'If you lose tomorrow night do you think your job's on the line?' This question was asked exactly one year to the day when we beat England.

"It made me think, 'Is it worth it? What can you do and you're still asked that question?'"

On the morning of the Spain game *The Sun* printed a front-page story about David Healy, Keith Gillespie and Roy Carroll having a night out in Belfast five days previously after the defeat to Iceland.

NI JOURNALIST PAUL FERGUSON:

"I know for a fact that I and my sports writing colleagues in the Northern Ireland Football Writers Association wouldn't have done

that. I think someone had an agenda.

"Football writers in Northern Ireland down the years have had an excellent relationship with both players and management and as [Dr] Malcolm Brodie, who has covered nearly every Northern Ireland match since around 1954, would tell you we at times are the envy of journalists throughout the world because of that. We value our contacts, we know what makes a good story, but there's mutual respect between players and sports writers.

"Was it a huge story? Was it a major story that you had to break on the morning of a match? Let's just say that we wouldn't have done it.

"It came from a news journalist. To me it was a nothing story. In a news journalist's mind they thought, 'How dare three international footballers go out and party after their team has been humiliated at Windsor Park.' To me I'm glad that they let off steam, got it out of their system. Did I want them to sit back wallow in self-pity in their hotel rooms and be miserable and then get to training on Monday and be even more miserable? No.

"Obviously this journalist or this newspaper was trying to go down the England route, these players don't play for England.

"News journalists and sports journalists are a completely different kettle of fish. News journalists could not care one jot if it damaged our relationship with the squad."

NI CAPTAIN AARON HUGHES:

"On the morning of the Spain game someone tried to make a story about some of the lads going out on the Saturday night after a bad defeat and having a quiet drink. That was unfair because Lawrie had said, 'You've had a long week, have your evening off now, go see your families, do whatever you wanna do, as long as you're back tomorrow there's no problem.'

"They weren't breaking any rules or curfews, they were just relaxing after a hard week. It seemed like there were attempts to stir things up a little bit. We all went to training again on the Monday and Iceland was finished and forgotten about. Well, not forgotten, we had a chat about it, but then we moved on to look towards the Spain game."

6 SEPTEMBER 2006 – UEFA EURO 2008
QUALIFYING ROUNDS
NORTHERN IRELAND v SPAIN
WINDSOR PARK, BELFAST
RESULT: WON 3–2
(DAVID HEALY x 3)
ATTENDANCE: 14,500

ABOVE: Keith Gillespie takes on Raul.

NI COACH TERRY GIBSON:

"The Spain game is my favourite memory. We'd obviously beaten England and that was a massive win, but at that stage it could have been a flash in the pan, it could have been a one-off. It was important to go on to the next European qualification and carry on, improve and prove to people that we weren't just capable of that one win.

"I think Spain at the time were a better team than England and it was all there to play for. We lost to Iceland and that was a real low point because expectations were so high, but to come back and play a team as good as Spain, go 1–0 down, then we got

ABOVE: Team Northern Ireland moments before taking to the field against Spain.

back to 1–1, then we went 2–1 down, then we got back to 2–2, and then went on to get the 3–2 victory. In the whole grand scheme of things I thought Spain were the best team we played in the whole three years. We were behind twice and then came back and eventually won the game. To come back like that after Iceland showed what we were really made of.

"We had some criticism after the Iceland game and it was slightly harsh but no more than that in my opinion. We went into that campaign full of hope, full of expectation and probably a bit unrealistic but there's nothing wrong with that. We'd worked hard to get to that stage, people were hoping and expecting us to do

DAVID HEALY:

"I always hoped I would score a hat-trick against somebody for Norn Ireland and there's no better stage than Windsor Park against such a quality side as Spain. It was a special, special night and another very special occasion at Windsor Park.

ABOVE: Warren Feeney is determined to take control of the ball from Cesc Fabregas.
RIGHT: David Healy scores against the Spaniards.

well and that's what we wanted. I think if you lose 3–0 at home there is going to be a certain amount of criticism. From my point of view I just felt, that's how it is, you have to take the rough with the smooth, you can't be too sensitive about it really. But from a player's point of view we started again on the Sunday, everyone was bitterly disappointed to say the least and there was a real resolve to put things right.

"I know Lawrie felt the pressure because he felt the expectation levels were probably unrealistic and like any manager when your team loses you take it to heart."

ABOVE: Close friends Keith Gillespie and David Healy celebrate one third of David's amazing hat-trick.

BELOW LEFT: Steve Davis against Spain.

BELOW MIDDLE: Another brilliant goal from David Healy, celebrated by his team mates.

BELOW RIGHT: Warren Feeney puts up another battle to gain control.

"It's nice when you get on a run and obviously Lawrie gave me a lot of praise in the press and said I should be playing at a higher level. And that did give me a great boost.

"I just accepted Lawrie the way he was. He had a few run-in's with individuals and the media but he knew the way he wanted to go about things. The press were sometimes tough on the players but we backed Lawrie and we always knew that he would back us.

"Lawrie didn't always celebrate much when we scored and took it in his stride but that's probably why we were so successful.

"'He wasn't trying to please everyone, he was pleasing himself, the Norn Ireland public and the players."

NI SUPPORTER ALAN FERRIS:

"I never thought anything could match the England game and result. How wrong could I have been? A fantastic game, a brilliant result another master stroke by our leader Lawrie, a 3–2 victory for our wee country was beyond anyone's wildest dreams. I was mentally and physically drained after the match, we celebrated long into the night, this had been a better performance than the one against England.

"When Lawrie threw his coat into the crowd I felt it was an impromptu decision by him, a sharing of something personal with the adoring fans. I didn't see it as a farewell gesture."

I was no longer working for the IFA but was working privately for Lawrie. We decided from the start that my work would be restricted to England as I didn't want to step on the toes of former colleagues in Northern Ireland.

Therefore when Lawrie was on international duty I refrained from contacting him. But after the Iceland game I knew he would be very unhappy and so sent a text. I followed the Spanish game on Teletext, imagining the absolute ecstasy in Windsor Park when the final score was eventually displayed on the screen.

It wasn't until I spoke to Lawrie that I realised for him at least the evening had not been one of unparalleled joy.

ABOVE: Stephen Craigan can't believe the score!
BELOW: Lawrie at the final whistle during the Spain game.

ABOVE: Lawrie and his backroom staff congratulate King David and captain Aaron at the final whistle.

BELOW: The boys celebrate their victory over Spain.

LAWRIE SANCHEZ:

"I went to the Spain game in the wrong frame of mind thinking, 'Why am I doing this? What do you have to do as a team to get credibility?' One poor performance and no matter what we'd achieved in the previous two years it was written off. It was exactly the boom-and-bust reporting I had asked them nicely to refrain from.

"I could read between the lines and knew what they were thinking, with calls for my head. I felt the post mortems were being written.

"We won the game, the players did tremendously well, David Healy got his hat-trick. I thought, 'Nobody expected this after Saturday's result. This is England again.'

"And after the England game people had said to me I should get out because that was it, we would never be able to top it. I always remember Wycombe, having taken the team to the semi-final of the FA Cup, and there were 20,000 people in the ground calling me the next Martin O'Neill. And I stayed on too long at Wycombe and the crowds fell when all the euphoria had disappeared about the semi-final; and people said I should have gone after the semi-final because that was as far as they were going to go.

"So after Spain my thoughts were, 'Well, I had the chance to leave after the England game and my credentials would have been high. Perhaps I'd never get another chance after Spain.' The press wanted my scalp. Nobody thought we could top England, and Spain was a better result.

"I felt there was a lack of respect for myself and the team. I just threw my coat into the crowd, my thoughts were, 'Well that's it, let someone else deal with it.'

"I went to see the players to congratulate them and say well done. At half time we had equalised and I had told them, 'That's taken care of Saturday's performance. Now let's take care of the next 20 years,' because it was 20-odd years since they'd last beaten Spain and I knew we could have them.

"Then I spoke to Howard in our bunker. I just said, 'I've had enough.' He asked me to have a think about it. I said I would not do the press conference; I was going back to the hotel. We did not *row, and the players would not have known about it because we were away from the dressing room."*

NI JOURNALIST PAUL FERGUSON:

"My greatest memory has to be the night we beat Spain. We'd just come back from a heavy defeat to Iceland, we were bitterly disappointed, moral was low and yet we faced a team full of galaticos. You had Raul, Fernando Torres, some superb players from Valencia, Barcelona, Real Madrid and to be honest we outplayed them. We thoroughly deserved to win that match.

"To come back after going down it was just sensational and the manner in which David Healy took his goals and the manner in which the team played was not only a credit to themselves but a credit to the country. That one day in particular seemed to unite the whole country.

"There were some people out there who maybe said that England was a fluke, that England played very, very poorly that night against us. But Spain actually played well and we played better. That maybe couldn't have been said about England. But against Spain, this was a team that came over, needed the points, were desperate for the points. England the previous year had basically qualified, even though it was a tremendous result. But Spain were looking to pick up points, it was early in the campaign and to come back after such a dismal performance and result against Iceland the previous Saturday would be my abiding memory from Lawrie Sanchez's reign.

"My first job after the match was in the mixed zone to interview a number of players. At that time the players were a bit stand-offish, and in particular David Healy. There'd been the bad press report on the morning of the game in one of the national newspapers suggesting that three players out of the squad had been drinking champagne and carrying on at a Belfast nightclub on the Saturday after the defeat to Iceland. David and the two other players in question, Roy Carroll and Keith [Gillespie] obviously weren't happy with this press report and decided that the press in general were the enemy. This seemed to show through some of the other players and they were a bit stand-offish even

after the terrific victory over Spain. But to be honest that was to be expected.

"Lawrie has commitments with the BBC immediately after a game and then he comes to see the written media afterwards. We believed he was going to come and do his run-of-the-mill press conference and tell us what a fantastic, glorious night it had been, one of the best of his career, and then news filtered through that no, he wasn't coming out, he wasn't talking. And then rumours started to suggest that he'd had a huge row with Howard over the way the media treated him and he had offered his resignation. He was going out on a high, he was fed up with the media, they were totally against him, he was in a no-win situation with them.

"Howard Wells came into the press conference with the official comment that Lawrie Sanchez would not be taking his place and would not be conducting his usual post-match press conference. Then news filtered through from sources and contacts that Lawrie had made his way to the airport. That of course was untrue because he got a flight the following morning.

"But I believe from my sources that it was proved to be correct over the next few days that he did have a row with Howard and did offer his resignation.

"Nobody could have predicted what happened after the Spain game. After the Iceland match we expected, as most people did, if we got a draw out of the Spain match that would be a tremendous result. To get a victory, most people expected Lawrie Sanchez to come into the post-match press conference and say, 'Told you so boys, you should have faith.' That was the attitude we expected, to fight back at us rather than merely walk away.

"Lawrie Sanchez to us was a very, very strong character, a man of many principals and leadership so for him to walk away just like that was a major surprise and I think a lot of people were shocked. Certainly I didn't expect him to do something like that.

"In retrospect if he had carried out his plan and resigned he would have walked out on a great high but thankfully for the good of Northern Ireland football he stayed on and we had many more marvellous times and nights with him as manager."

ABOVE: Retreating up the tunnel and into the dressing room area.

NI CAPTAIN AARON HUGHES:

"After the game I didn't notice anything out of the ordinary. It wasn't until the next day I started getting phone calls asking me strange things."

DAVID HEALY:

"I didn't see Lawrie throw his coat into the crowd and didn't know about it until I read it in the press the next day. There was a lot on his mind, a lot of things going on. The players got a lot of stick after

102

the Iceland game, and about things that happened after the Iceland game. Lawrie deals with it in his own way.

'I keep myself tucked away at the best of times. There was never any feeling that his actions stole the limelight off my hat-trick. Other people might say that, but I wouldn't."

After my conversation with Lawrie I watched *Match of the Day*. For once they were actually giving valid coverage to the game, something I'd worked on improving while I was with the IFA. So often this programme, which is shown throughout the UK, concentrated on England, showed footage of Scotland and Wales and usually even the Republic, but barely mentioned Northern Ireland. Tonight Gary Lineker was beaming with excitement, talking about a brilliant match and Alan Shearer praised the brilliance of David's goals. There was no interview with Lawrie, and no mention of any problem.

NI SUPPORTER ALAN FERRIS:

"The press announcement the following day regarding Lawrie's future, in my opinion took the gloss off the victory and performance of the team. The country should have been celebrating one of our finest performances but sadly our thoughts turned to the possibility of losing our illustrious leader, he had delivered everything he had said that he was going to do. We wanted him and we needed him, we held our breath waiting for confirmation that he was to remain our manager."

Lawrie flew back to Berkshire in England the morning after the game and I drove over to his home where we spoke at length, together with his partner Claire. Over the next couple of days Lawrie spoke with advisors, friends, family and the IFA.

To everyone's relief Lawrie, spurred on by the massive backing he received from the fans, decided to stay on and independently decided to issue statements to the press and IFA website in addition to posting a personal message on the Northern Ireland supporters website *www.ourweecountry.com*

LAWRIE SANCHEZ:

"I decided that the freedom and access I had given the press, certainly with regard to myself, would stop. They all had my number, they could phone me. When they had to confirm a story or a rumour they would call me and I gave them what I could. The press called me at the drop of a hat but I said from now on I would be available only for official press conferences and no more."

13 UEFA EURO 2008 QUALIFYING GAMES
DENMARK AND LATIVA PLUS A FRIENDLY WITH WALES

One of the conditions of Lawrie's return was that I was taken on for the rest of the European campaign to manage all his personal contact with the media and it was something I was happy to do. However, with a new communications team in place at Windsor Avenue Howard was reluctant to do this. Eventually it was agreed I would return only for the Denmark and Latvia games but as things turned out I did remain on board until Lawrie resigned to take over full-time at Fulham.

I knew the IFA staff, players, backroom team, many of the supporters and all of the media. It was great to be back. And with responsibility only for the team's communications whilst on international duty as opposed to everything to do with the IFA, I stayed with them at the team hotel during home games as well as away matches. It gave me an even greater insight into their work and preparation.

NI CAPTAIN AARON HUGHES:

"When we met up again Lawrie mentioned it [the problem with the media]. He said, 'Look, at the end of the day you guys just get on with your football, that's what you're here for and that's what you're good at. That's the reason why we get these things because we're doing so well, that when we do get a bad result the disappointment's so much. In a way it shows how far we've come.'

"He said anything that had happened was between him and the media."

OPPOSITE: Lawrie at open training in Denmark.

RIGHT: Arriving at the team hotel in Copenhagen.

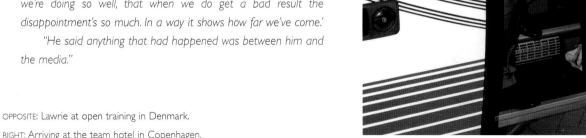

ABOVE: Lawrie arriving for training in Denmark.

BELOW: Terry Gibson and Lawrie Sanchez move the goalposts.

The team hotel in Copenhagen was beautiful, situated on the waterfront. While we conducted written media press conferences indoors we were able to provide UTV, BBC NI and SKY with a splendid backdrop as they interviewed Lawrie on the terrace.

Unsurprisingly, a large media contingent came out to Denmark. They stayed in an hotel just across the river from us and, on our first night in town, I went over to meet them. I trained and worked as a journalist for a long time before moving into PR and communications, and I understand the way the media work. Reporters on the ground do not write the headlines or the picture captions, that's the job of the sub-editors; reporters on tour are not away for a holiday, they work very hard and file a lot of copy often working late into the night to meet deadlines.

I had enjoyed a warm relationship with them all in my previous incarnation working at Windsor Avenue. Now I faced their wrath as they unleashed the frustration and anger they felt. My job was to be the conduit between them and Lawrie. They would not tolerate a short statement regarding the circumstances following the Spain game at the following day's press conference. They wanted the freedom to question

ABOVE: During a break in training Presseye photographer William Cherry takes a picture of Lawrie holding the IFA Christmas cards to put onto the IFA website.

ABOVE: The squad and backroom staff prepare for training.

ABOVE: Steven Beacom (*Belfast Telegraph*) and Ken Gaunt (Press Association) interview Grant McCann and Maik Taylor at the players' press conference in Copenhagen.

BELOW: Captain Aaron Hughes at the players' press conference.

Lawrie about his actions and it was agreed they could do so for the first part of the press conference. Fortunately after that everyone concentrated on the forthcoming match against Denmark.

The liaison officer appointed to us by the Danish FA was a charming man who expressed his admiration for the amount of preparation and serious training our boys put in. He told Lawrie after the game that a lot of teams came out just to relax and have fun, but we deserved our point because we had worked so hard for it.

NI SUPPORTER ALAN FERRIS:

"In the team hotel in Copenhagen as Lawrie was walking towards a reporter he stopped to talk to a few of us from the Bangor and Castlederg supporters clubs. We told him how delighted we were with his decision to stay, and yes we lambasted the press in a show of solidarity for our leader – how dare they criticise him.

"Lawrie shook our hands and thanked us for our support. He parted with the words, 'Enjoy the game and enjoy yourselves.' All 2,500 of us did, thanks to his drive and the performance of his team, another fabulous night."

ABOVE: Lawrie on the terrace at the team hotel in Copenhagen.

7 OCTOBER 2006 – UEFA EURO 2008
QUALIFYING ROUNDS
DENMARK v NORTHERN IRELAND
PARKEN STADIUM, COPENHAGEN
RESULT: DRAW 0–0
ATTENDANCE: 41,482

NI CAPTAIN AARON HUGHES:

"It was good to get my fiftieth cap in Denmark but it meant as much, if not more, that we got a valuable point there as well. There was satisfaction after the game that we'd gone to a hard place and come away with a good result.

"When we go back to our clubs now we don't get the stick that we used to. We get a little bit more respect now that we're getting good results."

ABOVE: David Healy, determined to take control of the ball against the Danes.

RIGHT: Being interviewed by SKY after the final whistle.

STEPHEN CRAIGAN:

"There were so many highs, a few lows for games where we drew or lost and thought we could have won. Beating England and Spain with Sweden still to come, it was a roller coaster an unbelievable journey. For me, a guy from Northern Ireland who dreamed of playing for his country, to be given an opportunity to play in these games, in front of a full crowd at Windsor Park and my family, and actually not just playing against them but competing and beating them it's something that will always stick.

ABOVE: NI defender Jonny Evans and Heather Jan Brunt at the Parken Stadium, Copenhagen after the final whistle.

ABOVE RIGHT: Lawrie and his son Jack at the post-match press conference.

RIGHT: The staff and players at Copenhagen airport waiting to fly home to Belfast.

BELOW: Former IFA president Jim Boyce with the fans after the 0–0 draw against Denmark.

"The one I always remember is Denmark. We had beaten Spain and there was a lot of hype, and to go to Denmark with a wee bit more expectation on our shoulders we were under a lot of pressure and to get a 0–0 draw was absolutely phenomenal. We defended well as a team and for myself I would class that as one of my better games. But just to be part of international football and playing against these guys is brilliant. It came down to Lawrie giving people an opportunity who might not have had an opportunity before. When he said, 'If you do the business you'll stay in the team,' that was something that drove me on and made me want to do well."

11 OCTOBER 2006 – UEFA EURO 2008
QUALIFYING ROUNDS
NORTHERN IRELAND v LATVIA
WINDSOR PARK, BELFAST
RESULT: WIN 1–0
(DAVID HEALY)
ATTENDANCE: 14,500

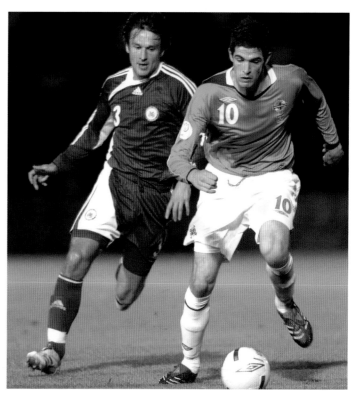

ABOVE: Kyle Lafferty in the Latvia game.

BELOW: David Healy having a shot at goal.

ABOVE: Sammy Clingan getting into the mood at Windsor Park before facing Latvia.

I had not witnessed the Spain game personally, but being back in Belfast the euphoria of that win was still evident. Although I had always travelled on the team bus to away matches I had never been on it for games at Windsor Park because, previously, I would have already been working at the stadium for hours before the team arrived. Now, as part of the travelling squad I shared their journey from the team hotel and as we approached Windsor the streets were fuller than I had ever seen them before, filled with the GAWA waving, laughing, cheering and apparently delirious with joy, wearing mad hats, frizzy green wigs and displaying enormous flags.

LAWRIE SANCHEZ:

"We came back from Denmark, which was tremendous, and the Latvia game was one where we needed to crystallise the points. We played better than the 1–0 score line suggests. To pick up four points from the two games was great. In the previous campaign after we'd beaten England we lost to Wales and Austria in the next two games; this time after beating Spain we showed how much we'd grown."

6 FEBRUARY 2007 – INTERNATIONAL FRIENDLY MATCH
NORTHERN IRELAND v WALES
WINDSOR PARK, BELFAST
RESULT: DRAW 0–0
ATTENDANCE: 14,000

The match against Wales may have been a friendly but it was of vital importance in the run-up to the next Euro 2008 qualifier in March.

Lawrie wanted to get a result, and with goal king David Healy absent due to a broken arm, and some other senior players also unavailable it gave a chance to youngsters. Strikers Peter Thompson (Linfield) and Dean Shiels (Hibernian), together with defender Sean Webb (Ross County), were back in the squad for the first time since the American tour.

LAWRIE SANCHEZ:

"We'd had a four month break, the big games started the next month, and this was a chance to get the lads back into Team Northern Ireland mentality, what we do, what we're good at, what has got us success.

"It gave me a chance to see players who hadn't perhaps had much grass time, because one or two of the more established players weren't there.

LEFT: Laughing with the players during training at Newforge prior to the International Challenge Match against Wales.

BELOW: Lawrie with goalkeeping coach Dave Beasant.

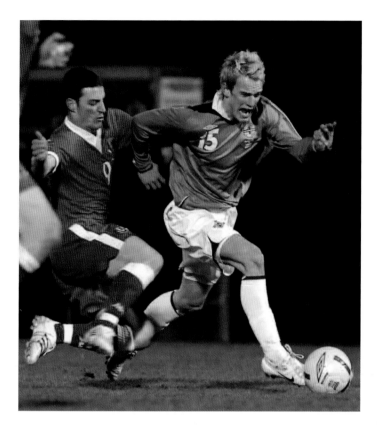

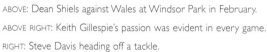

ABOVE: Dean Shiels against Wales at Windsor Park in February.

ABOVE RIGHT: Keith Gillespie's passion was evident in every game.

RIGHT: Steve Davis heading off a tackle.

"The youngsters did very well in training. It gave me a chance to see them perform for the first team. In the four competitive games we'd had so far we had a very tight squad, the only way to break in was through a friendly.

"The loss of David was a disappointment but I have always said as a manager, one man's disappointment is another man's opportunity. Now there was an opportunity for someone else to come in and perhaps fill those boots and show us something we hadn't seen before. Unfortunately, Warren Feeney, who would class himself as David's direct understudy, was also injured."

UEFA EURO 2008 QUALIFYING GAMES
LIECHTENSTEIN AND SWEDEN

Prior to flying out to Zurich the team met up in England for three days of training. Lawrie felt this would be the best preparation for two key matches, giving the players total privacy away from the intense glare of the media and fans, which would be amplified in a tiny country like Liechtenstein. I met up with them all at Heathrow. From Zurich we had a one-hour coach journey into Liechtenstein, it was very late at night so we saw nothing of the beautiful countryside. Our hotel, the Park Sonnenhof in Vaduz was small, intimate and family run, situated in the Rhine Valley of St Gallen with mountains and vineyards as a glorious backdrop, and the castle of Prince Hans-Adam II just a few hundred yards away. Liechtenstein is a constitutional hereditary monarchy and although I later discovered that Prince Hans-Adam and his guests sometimes ate in the restaurant of the hotel where we were staying, I also learnt that he rarely watched the national football team so wouldn't be at the match.

The players all had a huge meal on arrival, but I went straight to my room to unpack and found, as indeed was the case with all the rooms, a snow covered balcony overlooking the grounds. I listened to BBC radio on my laptop and heard the announcement that Bob Woolmer, the Pakistani cricket manager, had been murdered (this was later refuted), something which became a hot topic of conversation at the meal table over the next few days.

The following morning we took the team coach down to the astro turf pitch next to the Rheinpark Stadium in Vaduz. While Jon Goodman was taking the players for warming-up exercises, Lawrie and his backroom team had to shovel snow off the training pitch. They weren't too happy as they felt it should have already been done by the Liechtenstein FA and in fact Howard Wells (dressed for the weather in thermal long johns and a woolly pixie hat) went to complain to some of the ground staff about this and was told it had been cleared but more snow had since fallen.

Normally the first 15 minutes of a training session would be open to the press to take photographs and film footage, but for this session Lawrie had requested that they should come for the last 15 minutes. The media abided by this but unfortunately the continually falling snow and low temperature meant the session was cut short and they didn't get their pictures. To compensate Lawrie and the players spent quite a long time giving individual interviews before boarding the coach.

After lunch we had the press conferences. Lawrie first then Aaron our captain. All went well, and BBC NI also conducted an interview with Lawrie against a backdrop of the snow-covered mountains for a special segment on *Football Focus*. In the evening we went back to the stadium for another training session; it was quite modern and as it held only 6,000 and we had 3,000 travelling fans with us we knew a special atmosphere could be guaranteed.

WARREN FEENEY:

"We had some good snowball fights in Liechtenstein. Coming off the coach Lawrie got cracked on the back of the head with one.

OPPOSITE: Lawrie enjoying the scenery at the team hotel prior to playing Liechtenstein.

"On the morning of the game we went for a walk together. And Lawrie and Gibbo were hiding and throwing snowballs back at us. You wouldn't expect the manager to get involved in anything like that but it rubs off on the players and lets them relax and have a bit of a laugh. Lawrie was right there in the middle of it."

24 MARCH 2007 – UEFA EURO 2008
QUALIFYING ROUNDS
LIECHTENSTEIN v NORTHERN IRELAND
RHEINPARK STADIUM, VADUZ
RESULT: WIN 4–1
(DAVID HEALY X 3, GRANT McCANN)
ATTENDANCE: 4,340

ABOVE: The players made sure they had plenty of fun in the snow of Vaduz. Here Maik Taylor throws a snowball at one of his team mates.

ABOVE: Lawrie at his press conference in the team hotel the day before facing Liechtenstein.

RIGHT: Lawrie was still briefing the players as they lined up for the team photo at the Rheinpark Stadium in Vaduz.

I remember that night in Liechtenstein David was more excited about Grant's goal than he was about his own hat-trick. He had been substituted towards the end of the game and was in the dressing room, and came running out with joy when Grant scored.

DAVID HEALY:

"I was just so pleased. I grew up playing in the same boy's club as Grant. I was pleased that someone else had scored for Norn Iron, people were wondering if I was the only person who could score for Norn Ireland. For Grant to pop up, his mum and dad were so proud, to score was something very special for him."

Back at the team hotel the players enjoyed a late night feast. I didn't join them. I felt honoured to be a part of the backroom staff, but there were times I felt it was inappropriate for me to be around. The victory belonged to the boys and the coaching staff.

When we left the next morning our departure from the hotel was delayed as the staff did a sweep of all the vacated rooms and rushed out to hand over phones, MP3 players and boots that the younger players had forgotten to pack. The coach took us on a beautifully scenic

LAWRIE SANCHEZ:

"The hat-trick was typical David.

"We huffed and we puffed in the first half and hadn't blown the house down. And then Kyle Lafferty had a shot at goal that was rebounded off the 'keeper and then David put that in. It eased everybody, the fans, the players, it relaxed the field and David went on to complete his hat-trick.

"To be fair the best goal of the night was scored by Grant McCann, a cracking move straight off the training ground; a great diagonal from the left to Gillespie who drove to the by-line and delivered a terrific cross to the far post for Grant McCann to attack and head a fantastic goal."

ABOVE: Keith Gillespie is determined to hang onto the ball against Liechtenstein.

LEFT: Jonny Evans heads the ball to safety away from Liechtenstein 'keeper Peter Jehle.

BELOW: The score says it all.

journey through the countryside to Zurich airport where we boarded a chartered aeroplane back to Belfast.

By this stage David, with his second hat-trick, was joint top goal scorer in the whole competition alongside Germany's Lukas Poldolski, each with a tally of seven goals. Northern Ireland was standing second in Group F beneath our next opposition, Sweden, who remained unbeaten. I prepared a press release to this effect and handed it out during Lawrie's press conference on the Tuesday afternoon. As soon as we were finished I jumped into a taxi and went to the Stormont Hotel where the Swedish team were holding their own press conference.

I came back with the expected Swedish team formation, which was handed over to the Northern Ireland press and then to myself by visiting Swedish journalists. At our evening meal I gave it to Lawrie.

ABOVE: Keith Gillespie, Steve Davis and Lawrie Sanchez celebrate the 4–1 win over Liechtenstein.

Match days were sacrosanct and nothing had to disturb the players preparation. They would not normally train, going instead for a walk together before resting in the afternoon. I would spend the day dealing with paperwork and responding to requests from supporters and the media.

Finally, we would all meet up in the foyer of the hotel to board the team coach. This was my favourite part of the whole Team Northern Ireland experience. Lawrie always sat in the front seat, with his backroom and support staff spread across the seats behind him, then the players would sit sometimes together or sometimes on their own throughout the rest of the coach.

Two policemen on motorbikes would be waiting to escort us down the road and lead us into Belfast. As the engine started and the coach pulled out of the hotel grounds Lawrie would instruct the driver to switch on the DVD player; rousing music would play as we watched a brilliant compilation of all the best bits from former games, created by BBC editor Gareth Fitzsimons. I can only imagine what this did to the players, all I know is that I was so moved I felt either close to tears or wanted to jump off the bus and pull on a strip as soon as we got to Windsor Park to get out and play on the pitch.

As we approached the centre of Belfast off the M2 motorway, the police motorcyclists would occasionally flash their lights and weave in amongst the traffic, blocking off carriageways and stopping traffic to allow the coach to move on in its journey. When we drove down Royal Avenue towards Belfast City Hall in Donegall Square the streets full of shoppers would sometimes stop and stare, and as they slowly realised the coach contained their heroes they would clap or wave and get out their camera phones to record the moment. What a privilege it was to be a part of it all.

The boys didn't sing or get excited on the journey. Lawrie often told the press what a quiet bunch the team were. But in their own way they were all preparing for the task ahead.

NI SUPPORTER ALAN FERRIS:

"The wins against Latvia and Liechtenstein set us up for a massive game against Sweden, whoever won was going top of the group. Forty-five minutes before kick-off Windsor Park was packed, the Kop, indeed all of us, had hope. We had defeated England and Spain, we knew we could defeat Sweden. Optimism was high, for the first time since 1985 the fans believed we could beat one of Europe's top teams, the atmosphere was electric as the teams took to the pitch. We knew Lawrie and his staff had done their homework, the players were going to do their part, but we knew it was up to us the GAWA to ensure that we provided the twelfth man.

"Lawrie and the players always said the fans played a major role in the game. Our behaviour was always impeccable and vociferous support amazing, how so much noise is generated is beyond belief. I have attended many Premiership fixtures including the Man United AC Milan semi-final of the Champions League whenever 76,000 people were there but nothing compares to the sound of the GAWA in 'full tilt' to coin a wee Ulsterism if I may."

LAWRIE SANCHEZ:

"I was always thinking about ways to stimulate the lads, getting them into the right frame of mind. It's hard sometimes for players to come in from their club where they might be fighting relegation or promotion into a longer-term competition with big gaps between meetings.

"At our first training session in Bisham Abbey in England prior

to us flying out to Zurich I gave them a league table titled, 'What if?' and it showed us top of the table, with Sweden second, Denmark third, the way in fact that the group ultimately turned out.

"I passed it out and said, 'Take this with you, stick it in the bottom of your bag, think about it, talk about it. This is what can be achieved.'

"With the two wins we produced that table in reality. It was something just to stimulate the players and I'm sure one or two of them, when they got home from their trips, going through the bottom of their bags and plucking out this paper would see it was exactly as the table turned out."

28 MARCH 2007 – UEFA EURO 2008
QUALIFYING ROUNDS
NORTHERN IRELAND v SWEDEN
WINDSOR PARK, BELFAST
RESULT: WIN 2–1
(DAVID HEALY X 2)
ATTENDANCE: 14,000

NI SPORTS MASSAGE THERAPIST PAUL PRENTICE:

"Warren took a knock early on in the game and had to get treatment on his eye by the doctor. I think he did have to get a few stitches to stop the blood so that he could play on. Knowing Warren it wouldn't have mattered to him, he just wants to be out there playing. It wouldn't have mattered if half his head was hanging off he still would have gone out and headed the ball because he's got that type of spirit."

NI CONDITIONING COACH JON GOODMAN:

"I remember watching Northern Ireland beat England on the television and that probably still remains the greatest night, but to have experienced the Spain night and finally the Sweden victory was something I'll probably never experience again. The atmosphere at Windsor Park is the best thing about being with Northern Ireland."

NI CAPTAIN AARON HUGHES:

"Getting to the top of Group F was one of the highlights of my international career so far because at the start, like always, we were amongst the bottom seeds. It's so hard to make an impact when you've got four or five teams above you who are all better than you.

"After the start we had against Iceland, for everyone to pick themselves up and go in there, maybe it gave us a kick up the backside.

"To be top, you couldn't ask for anything better than that."

DAVID HEALY:

"At that stage there had been nothing better for me in my international career. To be top of the group and beat Sweden, another class side. We deserved to win the game."

NI SUPPORTER ALAN FERRIS:

"It was with pride that I looked at the group tables and saw our wee country sitting on top as indeed did every other member of the GAWA. We knew that it was a temporary measure but hey, make hay when the sun shines! We were top and we were going to enjoy it! With David Healy being the leading goal scorer among Europe's finest goal scorers it typified our performances and achievements and I was loving it.

"It is now cool and trendy to be a Northern Ireland supporter with the shirts seen everywhere.

"Many of the Northern Ireland songs were in existence prior to Lawrie's reign, however one song stands out head and shoulders above the rest, the GAWA's version of 'Amarillo' although only a couple of thousand know the GAWA's version:

Is this the Way to Northern Ireland?
If it is I will keep smiling
Dreaming dreams of Northern Ireland
And the boys in green who play for me.

"It is such a happy-go-lucky song, at Old Trafford it was played at half time when 6,500 members of the GAWA went crazy. After the victories against England, Spain and Sweden it was played over the PA system at Windsor. They were such happy nights!"

At the end of the match Lawrie sat in the boot room for a very long time while I waited in the corridor outside to take him to the post-match press conference. David's club manager Dennis Wise came down and joshed with Lawrie, Dave Beasant and Terry Gibson, all old Wimbledon mates together. Dennis had been quoted in the press recently feigning annoyance towards Lawrie over his publicly expressed surprise that no Premiership club had come in for David.

David was clearly pleased that his club manager had come to watch him. Dennis wanted to see what it was that made David so successful with Northern Ireland. When he scored during the match the fans sang to him: 'Are you watching Dennis Wise?'

I saw grown men cry that night. IFA vice president Raymond Kennedy (now president of the IFA) came towards me in the corridor outside the dressing room with tears in his eyes, wrapped his arms around me and kissed my cheeks.

The country was now top of Group F in the UEFA Euro 2008 qualifying tournament and David Healy was indisputably leading goal scorer. Northern Ireland was making history in more ways than one.

This was the week political unity had been reached with Ian Paisley and Martin McGuinness agreeing to power share at Stormont, so the country was in the headlines all over the world. Now, at home and even across the United Kingdom, the Northern Ireland football team would add to that feel good factor taking many back-page headlines.

Lawrie eventually came out of the boot room and we went to the press conference. He spoke at length to the daily papers, the Sundays, the radio and TV crews. Everyone was so happy. It is probably best that at the time none of us knew it would be the last time we would all be working together sharing such a special night at Windsor.

By the time we'd finished Lawrie and I had to rush to get onto the team coach to go back to the team hotel. It was practically empty. Most of the players go to the homes of their parents or other relatives at the end of a double header. The ones who come back to the team hotel are generally those without family still living in Northern Ireland. Lawrie sat at the front with his son Jack; his partner Claire came to sit beside me. Through the darkness of the night we wound our way back up the M2, past Samson and Goliath, our heads filled with victory.

TOP LEFT: Despite a cut to his eye which required stitches early in the game, Warren Feeney returned to the field to play an important part in the match against Sweden.

TOP RIGHT: Damien Johnson takes on Fredrik Ljungberg.

LEFT: High kicks from David Healy against Sweden's Olaf Melberg.

ABOVE: King David was named official highest goal scorer in the UEFA Euro 2008 tournament following his goals against Sweden.

ABOVE RIGHT: Kyle Lafferty chasing the ball.

RIGHT: David turns to celebrate his goal against the Swedes much to 'keeper Andreas Isaksson's despair.

Everyone felt immense pleasure and pride, going into the long summer on such a high. There wasn't another game until the middle of August, when Liechtenstein were due in Belfast. Even though other international matches in June might see Northern Ireland temporarily toppled from the top spot everyone was convinced our rightful place would be restored when we rejoined the campaign after a blissful summer.

15 FULHAM AND RESIGNATION

Northern Ireland supporters were determined to enjoy their new, elevated position in European football and under normal circumstances the announcement of the new FIFA rankings published on Wednesday 18 April 2007 would have been received with great rejoicing.

The new ranking of 33 confirmed a spectacular rise of 91 places since Lawrie had taken over in January 2004 when the country was ranked at its lowest ever at 124.

But the previous week another, rather more pressing announcement was reaching the ears of Northern Ireland fans. Their manager had been appointed caretaker manager of English Premiership club Fulham FC based in south-west London with the brief to save the club from relegation. The news made television, radio and newspaper headlines in Northern Ireland and England.

LAWRIE SANCHEZ:

"Over the Easter weekend I was on holiday in Austria with my family. We were skiing, staying at a lovely hotel. When we got back I thought, 'Wouldn't it be nice to be going back there next year for the European Championship finals.'

"We got back home Tuesday 10 April, watched a bit of TV, then I got a call from my agent saying that Fulham were interested,

would I be interested in doing the job? Chris Coleman had been sacked, and I said, 'Yes I'd be interested in talking to them.' I drove down to Harrods and met the chief executive and the chairman Mohamed Al Fayed and was offered the job and accepted it.

"The IFA were happy with it, and it was literally a 32-day deal, see it through the five games, no commitments on either side, show us what you can do."

NI JOURNALIST PAUL FERGUSON:

"I received a phone call at ten to 12 at night from my colleague Mark McIntosh telling me to switch on the SKY Sports News immediately. I was taken aback because everything seemed to happen so quickly. Chris Coleman was sacked, Lawrie took his place. My phone didn't stop ringing for three hours after that. Then I had a few media interviews to do with different radio stations."

NI CAPTAIN AARON HUGHES:

"I saw it announced on TV. I didn't think anything of it although a lot of people were speculating early on. I was asked if I thought he would stay on as Northern Ireland manager, and I felt if Fulham offered him the full-time job it would be very hard for him to turn down which is fully understandable."

Lawrie was officially unveiled to the media by Fulham on the Friday at their training ground in New Malden which is spread across several acres and once belonged to London University. At the centre is a substantial house now converted into offices, academy lecture rooms,

OPPOSITE: Victory over Sweden saw Northern Ireland top Group F in the UEFA Euro 2008 qualifying tournament. Left to right: Alan Mannus, Ivan Sproule, Sean Webb, Steve Davis, Chris Brunt, Grant McCann, Stephen Craigan with Michael Duff in front.

ABOVE: Chris Baird and Stuart Elliott celebrate Stuart's goal against Azerbaijan at Windsor Park – which together with Warren Feeney's penalty later in the game saw the first win at home under Lawrie's reign. The delight in the stadium was palpable.

the communications department and a room which looks to have originally been a grand dining or morning room and is now used for press conferences. Not particularly large, it has a fireplace, long sash windows and French doors opening to the grounds. A sponsor's backboard is set up permanently along one wall, with a table and two chairs in front of it. Beyond that are three rows of chairs, with space at the back for television cameras to set up.

A contingent of Northern Ireland media, including Stephen Watson (BBC NI), Adrian Logan (UTV), Paul Ferguson (*Sunday Life*), Stephen Looney (*Sunday World*), freelance Mark McIntosh and Graham Luney (*Belfast Telegraph*) had arrived to see their manager in his new role.

Lawrie was told the press conference room was too small to hold the large turnout of media, therefore two conferences would be held, one for the English media and then a separate one for the Northern Irish media. In both of them he insisted that if he kept Fulham up and was offered the job full-time he would remain as Northern Ireland manager.

NI JOURNALIST PAUL FERGUSON:

"We arrived early and the reception we received from Fulham was not cordial. We didn't receive a very warm welcome. We were told we could not wait in the waiting room so we had to go down to the town centre. Then of course we were not allowed into the main press conference, to be honest unlike some of my colleagues I had no major issue with that. My job was to get comments off Lawrie Sanchez regarding Northern Ireland and that's what I got that day.

"I looked at Lawrie and I thought, 'This is where you want to be, you look as if you are content here, even after a few days.'"

LAWRIE SANCHEZ:

"I said I felt I could combine both jobs and I meant it. That was my initial reaction. We'd come so far with Northern Ireland, it was something I wanted to complete, just six more games and we had a great chance of getting there.

"But the Fulham job was too good an opportunity to turn down. The fact that it was for a month gave them the chance to see if they liked me and if I could do the job. I set an objective which was to survive relegation, I did that, we got over the finishing line.

"During the course of that month it became clear that it's 24/7 being a Premier League manager and combining it with 24/7 as an international manager during those international periods would have been very difficult.

"The pressures on me would have been intense. If I lost league games prior to going and coming back from international duty, and during the international European campaign, one or other or both sides could claim I wasn't concentrating on my job. And the fact is you can't win every single game.

"When push comes to shove I had to make a decision

ABOVE: Lawrie with his Fulham backroom staff, Terry Gibson and Dave Beasant.

whether I was going to stay a Premiership manager or give that up and finish the job I had started with Northern Ireland. Ultimately, I decided that the Premiership was where I'd always said I wanted to manage and even if we did qualify for the Europeans there was no guarantee another club of Fulham's calibre would say, 'Here you are, clean sheet. Create your own team in the Premiership.'

"It was very, very tough and it's been reported that it showed in my face at the press conference, but I had to make the decision career-wise."

When Lawrie was appointed caretaker manager he had taken Terry Gibson and Dave Beasant with him to Fulham. In fact Dave had already been there, working for the previous manager Chris Coleman, and technically lost his job when Chris was sacked. But Lawrie reinstated him with immediate effect. Les Reed, who had been involved with Northern Ireland in a consultancy role during the Azerbaijan and England games, became technical director.

When Lawrie resigned as Northern Ireland manager on Friday 11 May 2007 his backroom staff, Terry, Dave, Jon Goodman and myself, effectively lost our role with the team. The Belfast-based personnel – Doc, Terry, Derek and Paul – who had worked under several managers for many years of course remain.

Terry, Dave and Les were appointed in fulltime positions with Lawrie at Fulham. After two very successful years with Reading Jon, who lives 80 miles from the club, decided to leave and concentrate on his own football fitness consultancy based in Loughton, Essex.

FORMER NI COACH TERRY GIBSON:

"I felt very sad, still do. It's been two months now but I still feel very, very sad. I wish I could have continued in some way. It was an adventure, I loved every minute of it. I got to meet some great people along the way, the players, the staff we worked with. People like Jim Boyce and Howard [Wells], there was always support from them and they appreciated the good work we were doing and they certainly showed their appreciation.

"For it all to end so suddenly it was strange. It all came out of the blue with Lawrie and Fulham, we didn't know how it was going to go in the month, then all of a sudden Lawrie's resigned and it was strange. I hadn't resigned and I didn't get the sack but it was just one of those things and you have to go along with what happened.

"It would have been fantastic to have kept involved for the last six games, just to see where the adventure was going to take us, hopefully it'll take them all the way to the European Championships and I really do believe that they can do it. I would have loved to have been involved. I made some great friendships with some of the players and you can see them giving it their all, they've all got ambition and aim to qualify.

"I hope to go over to Belfast because I didn't get the chance to say goodbye. I will bump into players along the way while we are at Fulham but I'd like to have the opportunity to say goodbye to the staff that we worked with. I've spoken to David Currie and Terry [Hayes] but I'd like to see the doctor, Derek and Paul.

"I'd like to thank them for the support they gave us because

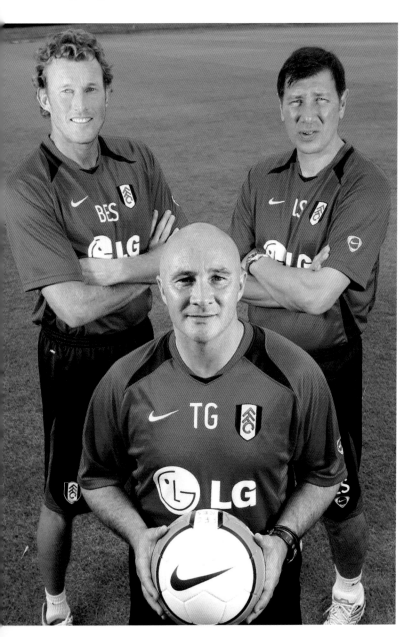

ABOVE: Dave, Terry and Lawrie at Fulham's training ground in Surrey, England.

they made me feel welcome right from the start, it impressed me because I was an English bloke, a little bloke from London and they took to us straight away so it would be nice to go over and say my goodbyes properly.

"If England and Northern Ireland both qualify for the European Championship I will support Northern Ireland 100 per cent. It's in my blood now, it's in my heart, it will always be there, I've got nothing but great memories there. I met some fantastic people, had some fantastic support, we were backed all the way 100 per cent by everyone involved and I will never ever forget my time involved with the Northern Ireland national team."

JAMES QUINN:

"Terry Gibson was more like one of the lads, he seemed to spend more time with us than he did with Lawrie and Bes [Dave Beasant]. Terry Gibson was my hero. When I was about seven I had 'Gibbo' sprayed with a blue spray can on my Dad's garage. He played for Coventry City at the time, my club. My earliest memory of football is Terry Gibson scoring goals, I just wanted to be like him, although obviously I grew a bit taller! Working with Terry was brilliant, he's one of the nicest fellas I've met in football."

After Lawrie's resignation press conference we went back to his office at the New Malden training ground to prepare a statement for the IFA website. Lawrie had to change out of his tracksuit and into a suit and tie for a meeting at Harrods with Mr Al Fayed, so we had little time to talk. After he left I spent time with his Fulham PA Jaki and Dave Beasant. Dave seemed as shocked as I was, and spoke on the phone to David Currie while I emailed Lawrie's statement to Howard Wells for approval.

I stayed down at Fulham for a couple of hours before finally driving back home, tackling the M25 circling London, four lanes of almost stationary traffic and found myself thinking of Denise and those early days when I first started working for the IFA and laughed as she complained about the traffic in central Belfast.

It took me two hours to get home and I hadn't been there long

when Lawrie called to discuss his statement for the fans website, www.ourweecountry.co.uk, Martin Harris helped me to locate Jim Rainey of the Amalgamation of Official Northern Ireland Supporters Clubs to get the statement live.

NI JOURNALIST PAUL FERGUSON:

"It was very clear from the outset that discipline was a major factor in Lawrie Sanchez's squads. He wanted to mould a squad the way he saw fit. He was firm but fair. He didn't want the players to like him but he wanted the players to respect him.

"When the Northern Ireland players went out to play they weren't playing for Lawrie Sanchez, they were playing for Northern Ireland and the fans. Lawrie Sanchez instilled right from the offset, even before Norway, a genuine belief and desire to play for your country. It wasn't just a case of showing up, getting your cap, he made them believe they could be credible in world football.

"He was the manager the boss, he didn't want to be like some managers in the past, and I'm not just talking about Northern Ireland here I'm talking about at club level over in England and Scotland, he didn't want to be one of the boys. That's why he had Dave Beasant and Gibbo, they were the link between the manager and the players. Of course there was a great relationship between David Healy and Aaron Hughes and the manager but deep down the players were playing for themselves, Northern Ireland and the fans. I honestly believe as long as they put in the performances Lawrie didn't give a damn whether he was liked or got on with certain players.

"I never had a problem with Lawrie Sanchez, I would actually go as far as to say I had an excellent professional relationship with Lawrie Sanchez from the start. I used to phone him regularly, usually once a week, he always answered my calls, if he didn't I left a message and he always returned my calls. And this was sometimes on a Saturday evening, an unsociable time for him maybe but an important time for myself to get the paper out. We did have our differences, like the US tour, sometimes he didn't like my questions but all I was looking for from him was a comment and if he said, 'No comment,' I respected that.

"I was sitting at my desk at work when I heard Lawrie had resigned as Northern Ireland manager. I received a phone call from a colleague saying that he believed Sanchez had resigned and then it flashed up on SKY Sports News. I have a TV right beside my desk. And then the phone calls started, interviews, helping out other papers, especially from England. I would say those were some of the busiest days in my career, Lawrie going to Fulham and then actually resigning. Weekends were ruined, I didn't have a weekend.

"First and foremost I am a Northern Ireland fan and I want the best for my country. So my first thoughts when Lawrie resigned and took the Fulham job full-time were that he'd done a tremendous job getting us to the top of the group and that it was a major pity that he would not be there to finish off the job.

"My second thought was, 'You have to take it.' If you're offered X amount of money compared to the Y amount of money that Northern Ireland were offering it's a no-brainer. Premiership football was his dream, he'd talked about it for some time, Northern Ireland simply could not compete, no matter what anybody says, with the lure of the Premiership and the amount of money he was going to receive. Although to be honest I don't think money was a major player in it, it was the lure of the Premiership and managing against some of the greatest managers in the world.

"The writing was on the wall the minute he took on the job of caretaker manager at Fulham. If he kept Fulham up and they offered him the job full-time there was no way he was going to turn them down. He'd always been very honest with us saying he wanted to get back into club management and at the highest level possible.

"I differ from some of my colleagues. I actually don't believe he either lied to us or turned his back on Northern Ireland. I believe he wanted to do both jobs but when it came to it I think Fulham gave him an ultimatum and said you either have this job or you don't, you can't have both. And there was only one option he could choose and that was Fulham.

"When Sammy McIlroy was manager it was far from a delight to cover Northern Ireland football, you knew you were going to have to write negative match reports. It was a real job, a chore. Lawrie came in, but let's be honest Lawrie didn't have wonderful times the whole three years, I remember Canada, Malta, Poland at home, and

then of course Iceland. But I think results against the English, Spanish, Portuguese, Latvia more than make up for it. Covering Northern Ireland had turned full circle and it was actually a joy to report on. Even though the workload was a hell of a lot more because obviously people want to read about success and therefore more space was provided by newspapers and journalists had to work that little bit extra. But I certainly didn't mind. It was a joy to cover and it's always a lot easier to speak to players when they are winning.

"If Northern Ireland qualify for Euro 2008 next year I think Lawrie Sanchez will be in Austria and Switzerland even if he wasn't invited. If it is only to come and watch then yes I would like to see him there because he deserves a huge and immense amount of credit, which everyone knows about, for getting us to where we are.

"Lawrie Sanchez left on a high and he will always be revered as one of Northern Ireland's greatest ever managers through results. You only have to look at the reception that Lawrie has received in his visits to Northern Ireland over the last month [June], with standing ovations wherever he goes. He's looked upon and thought of very, very highly over here and will be for some time to come."

KEITH GILLESPIE:

"I'd just come back from training and it was on SKY Sport, on the ticker tape along the bottom. I think a lot of people were disappointed because he'd taken us so far but the opportunity of Fulham was too good to turn down. Some people in Northern Ireland were a bit hasty in what they said, that Lawrie should have seen it through to the very end, but what he's done is to put us into a situation where we have a really good chance to qualify. To get a job in the Premiership is a really big thing and I don't blame Lawrie one little bit for taking that job. Most Northern Ireland players and fans will remember the job that he did for us in the three and a bit years that he was manager.

"To come from Lawrie's first game when we scored against Norway, although we lost the match it ended the goal drought; to come from there to beating England, Spain and Sweden it's been like a roller coaster ride. The whole last three years has been

ABOVE: Lawrie shares a joke with Stephen Craigan and Steve Jones training in Chicago prior to playing Romania during the US Tour in May 2006.

fantastic to be a Northern Ireland player and for most people in Northern Ireland it's been fantastic to be a fan because the one thing Lawrie said he wanted to do was to bring the feel good factor back to Northern Ireland and he's certainly done that."

WARREN FEENEY:

"In my 19 caps I've only had about five or six starts and my goal scoring's not too bad. I want to continue and start more. Lawrie gave me a start in the Sweden game and I think I did well and I thought I had cemented my place, and then he goes and takes the Fulham job and someone else will come in with their own ideas.

"But it's a great opportunity for Lawrie and no one can fault him for choosing a Premier League job.

"I was in a supermarket doing the shopping and on my way back home when I got a text message from a friend saying: 'Lawrie Sanchez is the new Fulham manager.'

"Everyone wants to play at the top level and he wants to manage at the top level.

"Lawrie is very tactical, and it showed in the number of goals that we scored from set pieces; what he worked on with us on the training ground. He did so well for Northern Ireland and made sure he covered everything, all the little things.

"My favourite memory of Lawrie's time in charge was of winning games. It's such a great feeling coming in after the match and hearing the manager say, 'Well done lads you've got a result.'

"If one stood out in my mind it would be the night of the England game. What an achievement that was to beat England. That'll be a memory that will stick forever."

NI CAPTAIN AARON HUGHES:

"I saw it break on the news and inevitably I got about 20 phone calls from everybody informing me what had happened. I spoke to Steve Davis about it. Everyone who knew Lawrie knew it was too good an offer for him to turn down.

"Nobody could have been happier than I was with the way things happened over such a short period of time during Lawrie's time with Northern Ireland. When he first came in we weren't having the greatest of times then three years later, we were top of the group. I always believed we had good players and he got the best out of them.

"Those three years will definitely be up there with the highs in my life, especially with some of the games and hopefully there'll be a few more to come to add to them. But certainly as far as international football goes it's been the best time that I've had in my international career.

"I believe we can still qualify for the Europeans because we've shown what we can do up until now and there's no reason why we can't keep going. And we were told at the start around 20 points would qualify. We're capable of it and have as good a chance as we've ever had. We've got to believe.

"Lawrie hasn't left with any animosity or bad feeling among the players. There'd be no reason why if we qualified, he couldn't pop in to say hello in Austria or Switzerland next year, no one would be bothered about that. I'm sure that he wants to see us go on and do it. It's a job he started and set us up to do and I guess he would love it to see us there."

ABOVE: Keith Gillespie and David Healy celebrating on the night David scored a hat-trick against Spain at Windsor.

FORMER IFA PRESIDENT JIM BOYCE:

"I was absolutely devastated, especially for the team and the fans. But he has left a great legacy, climbing the FIFA rankings and Lawrie will always be welcome in Northern Ireland and I wish him every success at Fulham."

PHOTOGRAPHER WILLIAM CHERRY:

"Lawrie brought a more professional attitude to the team. He may not have been as sociable as other managers, but he is in the results game, and he certainly got results! He was certainly never unpleasant or unhelpful to me; in fact I can't think of a single occasion that he refused my requests.

"I feel privileged to be in the job that I have – to photograph the team I've grown up supporting, and to be part of the ups and downs. Lawrie has got us to a great position, meaning that I may now be able to photograph our wee country in a major championship final."

DAVID HEALY:

"Lawrie and I spoke a lot about football, not just about how the team would play, but about football in general. I always had a close relationship with Lawrie, we didn't speak every day but we spoke regularly and Lawrie understood how much playing for Northern Ireland means to me and he was always so good to me.

"When I heard that Lawrie had resigned first of all I was disappointed, but I understood why Lawrie wanted to go. By no means did Lawrie walk out on Northern Ireland, people say maybe we would have qualified if Lawrie had stayed, but at the end of the day it's still the same group of players and we're still in with a great chance.

"He goes with the greatest of blessings not just from me but, I'm sure, from the rest of the boys in the team. He had an opportunity he couldn't turn down, a chance to be in the Premier League. Like any manager, any player, everybody wants to be part of the Premier League. He's got a big job at a big club and a great chance to go and better himself."

STEPHEN CRAIGAN:

"I think that what you see of Lawrie in the press is what you get. He's a very private person. He let Jon Goodman, Terry Gibson and Dave Beasant take over the joking and laughing with the players. Lawrie was always the serious one who focused on the football.

"He always gave such positive team talks and made us believe we could beat anyone irrespective of names and reputations and it worked.

"If a player was asked to move up to a Premiership club of course he would consider that and would want to take the opportunity. Lawrie is a normal human being, he made a name for himself, managers move on results. If you look at his record over his three years with Northern Ireland it was only natural that clubs would be looking and be interested. I knew that if he kept Fulham up they would be interested in keeping him.

"It was a sad day for Northern Ireland football, we had some fantastic games and had pushed on but we have to give him credit

132

and respect. It was a massive disappointment but I think Lawrie would totally agree the players were involved as much as he was so we have to move on.

"I'm disappointed of course, Lawrie believed in me and was prepared to give me a chance to play for my country. Of course there is regret and I wish there had been an opportunity for him to see the job through, but the Premiership now is such a big, big job it wouldn't have been right for Lawrie to try and do two jobs.

"He's taken our country onto another level and I think anybody in Northern Ireland can only shake his hand, pat him on the back and wish him well because without him we wouldn't be in the position we are in."

IFA HEAD OF INTERNATIONAL ADMINISTRATION DAVID CURRIE:

"Lawrie was professional about his job and so am I so we were both looking for the same thing. I got on well with Lawrie, I don't think there were any times when we had any problems.

"There are a lot of memories. The Caribbean tour was fantastic we were undefeated, and the big results against England and Spain. There were more ups than downs, I really enjoyed it.

"Lawrie called me about an hour after his resignation was announced. And then I spoke to him a day or two later as well. I was sad to see him go, but as I said to him, I couldn't blame him for taking that opportunity. From a selfish point of view it would have been nice for us if he had seen out the campaign but people wouldn't hang about and wait for him and it's difficult to do two jobs at one time so I don't blame him one bit for taking up a job in the Premiership, which he always wanted to do. So I hope he does well there."

NI SPORTS MASSAGE THERAPIST PAUL PRENTICE:

"I first heard that Lawrie had resigned when I was driving to work, on a local radio channel. From a Northern Ireland supporters point of view it was a great blow because Lawrie brought so much to Northern Ireland football but I can totally understand why he left when he did.

"He never made any secret of the fact that he wanted to manage a Premiership club and frankly a man of his quality should be manager of a Premiership club. It was just unfortunate with the timing.

"He phoned me a couple of days after it went public. I think he was phoning all the staff, a courtesy call just to thank us for our work with the team and to explain his situation so that we weren't in any doubt. He was reluctant to leave Northern Ireland, I could tell that he had wanted to do both jobs but it just wasn't a doable option for him.

"When we worked together, on occasions when I was in the treatment room or just passing the time in general conversation he would bring up the well-being of the players and ask me who had been having treatment, whether I had regular people coming in to see me, the same faces. Sometimes he asked me about the level of injuries, but mostly he was just concerned that what I was there for, the sports massage, was of benefit to the players. If you ask any of the players they would agree that it was of benefit. Any player I ever worked with, I asked for constructive criticism if they had any and everything I got back was of a positive nature so I was happy that it was benefiting the squad, and that was the type of conversation I would have with him.

"We talked about other things too, small talk and general stuff. I found Lawrie to be a very nice man, very polite courteous person, he would never pass you without asking how you were."

KATE HOEY MP:

"I was disappointed. But I believe it was very difficult. I know that whilst he desperately wanted to manage a Premier League club he also would love to be taking a team to the European championships because to lead a national team at a big championship is a big thing for a manager.

"Given that he had put us well on the road to doing that I think it was disappointing for all of us, including him. But he has now got the best of things because if we go ahead and qualify people will always put it down to Lawrie because he changed us from being a team that had not scored a goal and was losing all the time to believing in ourselves again and winning. And if we don't qualify now Lawrie still comes out of it well. He personally can't lose by it.

"I know he has written to the London Northern Ireland Supporters Club to say that he would like to remain as president. They wrote to him to say they understood why he left but wanted him to remain as president. He wrote them a lovely letter saying that he would be following Northern Ireland and wishing them well.

"One of my favourite supporter's songs is 'We're Not Brazil We're Northern Ireland' and I think that's what makes us very special because we're not a big country. Although we have to have commercialisation and all of that I think we want to be successful in our own way and not just become a 'B' version of England with all England's traumas and player prima donnas. Someone like David Healy will come back home, to his own little town and it's true that whilst he's absolutely a hero he's still treated very much like, 'Well you're back home now and you're one of us.' And I think that's what makes our team so special.

"For years we were ignored. Northern Ireland would never get any publicity at all. If they were giving any kind of results we would be right at the end of the sports bulletins. The Republic of Ireland would always get pushed first even though it was a 'foreign country' and that really irked people. And now that is gradually changing because we are on the way up.

"Whatever happens to Lawrie in the future he gave the people of Northern Ireland a fantastic lift and made everybody proud again of the team, when actually we have a very proud history.

"It's really good to bring the good times back and when the history of Northern Ireland football is written, as it is periodically, Lawrie will be right up there as one of our great successes."

IFA HEAD OF OPERATIONS WILLIAM CAMPBELL:

"Without a doubt he brought something special to this country.

"Don't ask me exactly what it was because I don't think you can quantify what he did, but he created a great belief.

"Lawrie had a purpose. He knew what he was wanting to do. It took him a year to 18 months to get to grips with international football, it's different from the normal run of the mill stuff that managers are used to with clubs. It took him that first tournament to get into his stride but once he knew what he wanted and knew the players and how he wanted to play he was able to transfer that knowledge and belief to the players.

"It's the best spirit I've seen in the team since the 1986 squad. I started at the IFA in 1983 so I was with the 1986 squad in Mexico and I can see the same spirit today. I think probably on a player-to-player basis the '86 team was probably a better team player-wise, but as an entity the team today is certainly as strong if not stronger.

"I was sad to see Lawrie go because I think we were within touching distance of something quite remarkable. We still might be. And I'm sure Lawrie would have liked to stay and see it through. But once the Fulham job came up it was probably inevitable that it was going to end the way it did. It is hard to serve two masters.

"It was a particularly special three years."

FORMER IFA PRESS OFFICER DENISE WARD:

"I have great memories of traveling and working with the team, it was a great opportunity which I was very lucky to gain by chance as the previous press officer had retired. I had no doubt I was out of my depth being involved with the team but that didn't mean I was going to run away from that opportunity – who would? I am very grateful for the opportunities I was given – I truly hope that I keep my mind when I am older as I never want to forget how I worked alongside the Northern Ireland team, visited fantastic countries, met some fantastic people, got momentarily star-struck when I saw world class players and enjoyed time with highly regarded members of the press.

"Today, in 2007, Lawrie has put us on the map and earned respect for us. We were a bit of a joke for a few years before Lawrie, even the boys used to say they were getting ribbing from their club mates. Lawrie got respect for the boys. He's done a great job.

"It was sad to see him go but things like that can never last. Northern Ireland and the IFA have been victims of his success but without him they wouldn't be where they are now. I don't feel any bitterness that he had to go."

NI SUPPORTER ALAN FERRIS:

"Lawrie took us from the depth of depression, from our lowest position in world rankings, from a team that had not scored in over 1,298 minutes of football, let alone win a game, to a team that has made Europe sit up and take notice of our wee country. He has achieved his three goals and more, as one who enjoys a gamble I wouldn't have bet one pound if someone had offered me a bet on how or where Northern Ireland have gone since Lawrie's appointment. If I had have I would have been a very rich man, the odds were stacked against him and his team but he delivered the unthinkable.

"For me for our wee country to lose Lawrie as our manager and to lose Lawrie as a friend to the GAWA is a major blow. I firmly believe that he could have taken us to the finals next year. I was really disappointed when he resigned, I had hoped that he could have done both jobs in the interim but alas that was not the case. I respect his decision, what Lawrie Sanchez did for Northern Ireland football is well documented but words cannot describe the pleasure and pride he has given to me and the rest of the GAWA. His reign was like a roller coaster ride ups and downs but the ups far outweighed the downs. On a personal note I would like to congratulate him on his achievement with us, and thank him for the fantastic times he has given us. I have always been a Northern Ireland supporter but Lawrie, his staff and players put pride back in our national sport. It is now cool and trendy to be a Northern Ireland supporter. The sales of IFA merchandise have soared. Everywhere you go you see the famous green and white of our wee country Northern Ireland.

"To you Lawrie, sir, I thank you."

LAWRIE SANCHEZ:

"There were so many highs. There were some lows as well, but more highs. The best time for me was the feeling of satisfaction after the England, Spain and Sweden games. Just standing watching the players do their lap of honour in front of the crowd at Windsor. To see the elation on their faces, players who wouldn't

ABOVE: Chris Brunt, Kyle Lafferty and David Healy celebrate after one of David's three goals during the match against Liechtenstein.

have ever dreamed of doing that type of stuff. The Stephen Craigan's of this world who would give their right arm to play for Northern Ireland. Obviously you've got the stars of the team, everybody knows Healy, Gillespie, they're self evident but the solid players in the team, Duff, Craigan, to see them, through all their hard work, crystallise moments not once not twice but three times, and see them share that with the crowd. Just standing there with all my coaching staff all around me enjoying the moment. They were the best times for me."

EPILOGUE

ABOVE: David, Aaron, Lawrie, Chris and Steve at the Fulham FC training ground in New Malden, Surrey, England.

As manager of Fulham FC, Lawrie Sanchez signed Northern Ireland's captain Aaron Hughes, leading goal scorer David Healy, midfielder Steve Davis and defender Chris Baird to the Premiership club during June and July 2007.